CREATE 2D MOBILE GAMES WITH GAMES WITH CORONA SDK

Bound to Create

You are a creator.

Whatever your form of expression — photography, filmmaking, animation, games, audio, media communication, web design, or theatre — you simply want to create without limitation. Bound by nothing except your own creativity and determination.

Focal Press can help.

For over 75 years Focal has published books that support your creative goals. Our founder, Andor Kraszna-Krausz, established Focal in 1938 so you could have access to leading-edge expert knowledge, techniques, and tools that allow you to create without constraint. We strive to create exceptional, engaging, and practical content that helps you master your passion.

Focal Press and you.

Bound to create.

We'd love to hear how we've helped
you create. Share your experience:
www.focalpress.com/boundtocreate

Focal Press
Taylor & Francis Group

CREATE 2D MOBILE GAMES WITH CORONA SDK

For iOS and Android

DAVID MEKERSA

Focal Press
Taylor & Francis Group

NEW YORK AND LONDON

First published 2015
by Focal Press
70 Blanchard Road, Suite 402, Burlington, MA 01803

and by Focal Press
2 Park Square, Milton Park, Abingdon, Oxon OX14 4RN

Focal Press is an imprint of the Taylor & Francis Group, an informa business

Library of Congress Cataloging-in-Publication Data
Mekersa, David.
    Create 2D mobile games with Corona SDK : for iOS and Android /
David Mekersa.
        pages cm
    1. Mobile games.   2. Smartphones—Programming.   3. Android (Electronic resource)   4. iOS (Electronic resource)   I. Title.
    QA76.76.C672M4527 2015
    004.167—dc23
    2014034171

ISBN: 978-1-138-01409-1 (pbk)
ISBN: 978-1-315-79485-3 (ebk)

Typeset in Minion Pro
by Apex CoVantage, LLC

Contents

Acknowledgments   ix

Part 1: Lua   3

Get Prepared   7

Variables, Tables, and Expressions   11

Functions   17

Control Structure Statements   23

Arrays and Lists   29

Object-Oriented Programming With Lua   35

Part 2: Display   43

Texts   47

Images   53

Shapes   57

Part 3: Move   67

Move Objects Around the Screen: The Interactive Way   75

Move Objects Around the Screen: Frame by Frame   81

Make Them Fall: The Physics Engine   87

Make Them Collide But Not Fall   97

Animate Images With Sprites   105

Part 4: Advanced Features   113

Add Sounds and Music   121

Menu and User Interface   125

The Screen Jungles   135

Save and Restore Data   143

Part 5: To the Stores   149

Test and Debug   157

Debug   163

Deploy   169

More With Corona SDK?   177

Part 6: Epilog   183

Index   187

Acknowledgments

I would like to express my gratitude to the people who helped me during the writing of this book.

First of all, thanks to those that made this possible: Sean Connelly and Caitlin Murphy from Focal Press; they gave me their trust (and I gave them some delay, sorry about that!).

Thanks to my wonderful wife for her patience and encouragement: I did it, princess! Thanks to my amazing kids Clementine and Antoine: their admiration is pure energy, especially during the hard days when the doubt rode around.

Thanks to Florian Boeuf, my assistant at Casual Box, for pushing me every day to write one more chapter and get to the end.

Thanks to those who read over my early manuscript, caught the errors and gave me advice, especially Sebastien Charret and Caitlin Murphy.

A big thanks to Erin Bell, my proofreader. From my game Age of Enigma to this book, she's been a devoted and very accurate companion. Thanks Erin!

Last but not least, I would like to thank you who bought this book and are entering the amazing world of game programming. I hope you'll get the pleasure I had when I saw my first game come to life on my Amstrad CPC 464 some years ago . . .

How I Discovered I Could Learn a New Programming Language in Less Than 48 Hours!

Recently, while I was warming up to attend a Game Jam, I was thinking about how many programming languages and frameworks I had learned and used in my life as a coder. Here are some:

- *Locomotive Basic*
- *Z80 and Motorola 68000 Assembler*
- *GFA Basic*
- *Amos Basic*
- *Clipper*
- *Pascal*
- *C and C++*
- *Delphi (based on Pascal)*
- *WLanguage (WinDev)*
- *Visual Basic*
- *Java*
- *PHP*

- *JavaScript*
- *BlitzBasic*
- *Monkey X Basic*
- *Lua (for Löve 2D and Corona SDK)*
- *C Sharp*

More than 10 different languages and almost 20 if we include the different implementations (Borland Pascal and Delphi, for example, use the same language but must be learned individually).

After so much practice, I had built my own personal way to learn, which I'm going to share with you.

For this particular Game Jam, I decided to learn Löve (a 2D framework based on Lua). I knew the Lua language already, so it only took me few hours to be able to understand the framework and create a game prototype.

I had learned Lua using Corona SDK a few months before, and I just needed one day to learn the language plus the basics of the Framework and some advanced features!

Think it's impressive? You can do the same.

You just have to learn less and build a minimal toolkit. Let me explain!

Learn Less

This is a simple method based on common sense.

Learn only the basics, then start a real project.

The basics are:

- Minimum skeleton / minimal game engine
- How to run / test the code
- Variables, functions, classes and other language fundamentals
- Lists and/or arrays
- Display an image and make it move
- . . . That's all!

Depending on your skill level, mastering the basics of a programming language associated with its framework will take you between two hours and one day.

At this stage, you're not an expert, and it's not enough for the entire project you're going to work on . . . No problem! Start the project now!

You'll learn any additional concepts only when you'll need to use them.

Why is this method good for you?

1) It avoids learning useless stuff. Why learn this advanced API if you won't need it for your first project? You don't have to be an expert; you just need to know enough to produce something right now!

2) It keeps your motivation high with fast results and many small, early successes.

The Minimal Toolkit: The Magic 7

Now that you understand the basics, let's dig into the framework.

To be able to create your first game, you just need to master 7 things. You need to know how to:

1) Organize your app into different screens (menu, options, gameplay, etc.).
2) Display text and images.
3) Move and scale what you display.
4) Animate it.
5) Play sounds.
6) Take inputs (touch on mobile, keys and mouse on desktop).
7) Save the game state (optional).

It might not sound like much, yet with this minimal toolkit you can create some great classics: Pac-Man, Space Invaders, Tetris, Mario Bros., Street Fighter, Puzzle Bobble, Zelda, and many more!

In this book, I will teach you to create any kind of game with Corona SDK by following this method.

In addition to the lesson, each chapter will provide tips and links that take the concept even further.

It's time to make stuff!

Master
LUA

You are here

Part 1
Lua

Introduction to Script Programming With Lua

Before getting to the heart of the matter (coding!), let's learn what Lua means, what a programming language is, and two tips to code like a pro.

Moon

Lua means "moon" in Portuguese. It's pronounced "loo-ah" and not "L.U.A." It was created in Brazil in 1993 and is now available for a wide variety of systems.

Corona SDK uses Lua as its programming language. Because Lua is very easy to learn, it has allowed Corona SDK to become one of the most accessible tools to create mobile games and applications.

A Script Is a Shopping List

Lua is a programming language, and more precisely, a scripting language.

Think of a typical **shopping list**:

- look for butter at the store
- if there is no butter, buy margarine
- go back home

A script is no more than a shopping list **for a computer**!
Here is an example of our shopping list in Lua code:

```
result = LookFor("butter")
If result == false then
        MoveToStore()
        Buy("margarine")
        GotoHome()
End
UseButter()
```

It's not terribly realistic, but it'll help you to understand what a scripting language is.

Comments

Sometimes you'll need to explain something in your code that isn't part of the code itself. For example, leaving a note to yourself about something you have to remember, or providing information to others who might read your code.

To insert a comment just do this:

```
-- Here is a comment
```

If the comment is long, do it like this:

```
--[[
Here is a long comment.
It's amazing how this comment is long!
--]]
```

Some Advice Regarding Comments

- Use comments often! Several weeks or months later, you'll be happy to find these helpful reminders.
- A comment needs to provide information, not just repeat what the code already explains by itself. An example of a redundant comment would be:

```
-- Increase value (this comment is crap)
value = value + 1
```

- A comment is useful to deactivate a line of code temporarily. For example:

```
-- the line of code below won't be executed
-- value = 3
```

- Remove a comment when it is no longer valid.

Traces

On many occasions, you'll need to display something that's not for your users, but only for you. A kind of "I was here!" to check if your code is doing what you expect. (Yes, the code isn't always obedient!)

Here is how to display a trace:

```
print("David was here!")
```

This instruction will display "David was here!" in the console when this instruction is executed.

The console is a kind of ticker that's essential to your survival.

> **TOP TIP:** Traces are the best and simplest way to discover bugs and fix them. It's like having a spy in your code! You'll learn more about traces in the chapter addressing debugging.

That's All

That's enough to start. Let's now look at Lua in detail!

Get Prepared

We all love action. So, before we learn anything, let's install Corona SDK! You'll then be ready to enter the code from the examples and test them.

Installing Corona SDK

Corona SDK is, as its name suggests, a software development kit: a mix of tools that allow developers to create certain applications.

To enter and test our code, we'll use the Corona Editor (which is based on a text editor called Sublime Text 2). We call this tool an IDE (Integrated Development Environment), from which you'll enter code, compile, and launch your apps for testing.

Sublime Text is an amazing tool, and it's the best choice from my point of view. You can use any text editor you like, of course, but you won't get the automated features such as completion, compiling, and so forth.

Installing the SDK is simple. Just follow the officially documented steps according to your operating system.

Installing Corona SDK for Mac OS X

http://docs.coronalabs.com/guide/start/installMac/index.html

Installing Corona SDK for Windows

http://docs.coronalabs.com/guide/start/installWin/index.html

Everything working fine? Now it's time to install the IDE.

Installing Corona Editor

The official Corona Editor page explains everything you need to know: http://coronalabs.com/products/editor/

To install the editor:

1) Install Sublime from www.sublimetext.com/ (we'll use Sublime Text 2).
2) Install the Package Control Plugin: follow the instructions at https://sublime.wbond.net/installation.

3) Choose: Tools > Command Palette . . . > Package Control: Install Package.
4) Find Corona Editor by typing in the search field, then click on it to install.
5) Restart Sublime Text or reopen any file with the extension *.lua to see the new features.

You're done!

> NOTE: Sublime Text 2 may be downloaded and evaluated for free; however, a license must be purchased for continued use. There is currently no enforced time limit for the evaluation.

Experiment

In the next chapter, I'll teach you Lua.

Lua is the scripting language, not the SDK. It's quite independent from Corona SDK, but a good way to learn is to experiment with the examples and lessons through Corona SDK. This way, you'll become familiar with the Corona SDK tools.

How do you begin experimenting with Lua code?

1) Run Corona Simulator (you should have already installed it).
2) Choose: File > New Project.
3) Choose: "Blank" then click "Next."
4) Save the project in the directory of your choice.
5) Choose: "Open in Editor."

Sublime Text will open a new file, main.lua, with just few comments in it:

The Sublime Text editor in action.

Keep this open and jump to the next chapter. You're ready to learn Lua!

Variables, Tables, and Expressions

The starting point for any programming language is learning how to **store values and data**.

What are some examples? In a game you'll need to store things like a player's name and status, the number of lives, the score, the enemies, and the remaining time.

These values are from different **types.** For instance:

- A name is a **string**
- A score is a **number**

Store Simple Values

Simple useful types in Lua are numbers, strings, and Booleans.

To store a value of one of these types, you have to **name** the value and **assign** it.

Look at this:

```
title = "Rocky"
```

This gives a string the name "title" and assigns it "Rocky" as a value. Please note that **strings are between quotation marks**.

Numbers are expressed in the same way, except that the value does not use quotation marks:

```
lives = 3
```

Boolean values can only be *true* or *false*.

```
started = true
```

> IMPORTANT: The variable name has to start with a letter, and can contain letters and numbers, with no spaces.

Lua is case sensitive, which means that an uppercase "L" is different than a lowercase "l." In other words, these variables are not the same:

```
Lives = 3
lives = 3
```

Got it?

Please note that there is a special type to define the lack of value: **nil**.

```
myVariable = nil
```

> **IMPORTANT:** Lua will not check whether a variable you're trying to use was already assigned previously. In your code, if you try to access a nonassigned variable, Lua will consider the value as *nil*. Keep this in mind.

Store Complex Values

Lua is an amazing programming language in that it provides a sole "container" to store complex values.

Tables

To store more complex data, like a player, you'll use tables. Think of a table as a magic box. You give it a name, and then you put stuff inside. Here is an example of a table:

```
MyPlayer = {}
MyPlayer.Energy = 100
MyPlayer.x = 50
MyPlayer.y = 20
```

This short example demonstrates the creation of a table called *MyPlayer*, which contains 3 variables. A table is quite simple yet amazingly powerful, because it can contain variables as well as functions. We'll learn what functions are in the next chapter.

Expressions

Expressions will be absolutely everywhere in your code. However, I won't dig too deeply into expressions because I prefer practice rather than theory. Here are some basics to understand what they are.

According to Wikipedia:

> *An expression in a programming language is a combination of explicit values, constants, variables, operators, and functions that are interpreted according to the particular rules of precedence and*

*of association for a particular programming language, which computes
and then produces (returns, in a stateful environment) another value.*

Ouch! I ran out of breath! Just keep in mind that an expression
returns a value and is used to perform arithmetic or comparisons.
It should remind you of using a scientific calculator at school.
For arithmetic expressions, Lua supports these operators:

+ (addition)
– (subtraction)
* (multiplication)
/ (division)

Here is an example of an arithmetic expression, assigned to a variable
named *myResult*:

```
myResult = 1 + 12
```

To compare values, we use relational expressions. Lua supports these
relational operators:

< (less than)
> (greater than)
<= (less than or equal to)
>= (greater than or equal to)
== (equal to)
~= (not equal to)

Using relational operators will always result in *true* or *false*.

```
myResult = score > 10
```

In this example, *myResult* is a Boolean and will store *true* if *score* is 11
or more.
An arithmetic expression can combine numeric values and variables.
In the previous example, score is a numeric variable, and is compared to
a numeric value (10).

> NOTE: If you use a string in a mathematical expression, Lua will
> express its displeasure.

Expressions are nothing without statements, but we'll save these for later.

Practice!

In your main.lua file (refer to "Get Prepared" in the previous chapter), enter some expressions to experiment with variables in Lua. Just type in this code:

```lua
-- Your code here
name = "Rocky"
age = 30

print("My name is",name," and I'm",age)

-- Access to a nil variable
print("This unknown variable is...",
unknownVariable)

-- Complex values
MyPlayer = {}
MyPlayer.Energy = 100
MyPlayer.x = 50
MyPlayer.y = 20

print("The player is at:")
print("x:",MyPlayer.x)
print("y:",MyPlayer.x)
print("And its energy level is",MyPlayer.
Energy)
```

Now, press Command+b (Mac) or CTRL+b (Windows) to execute your code. The console is displayed in the bottom of Sublime Text and should contain:

```
My name is   Rocky   and I'm     30
This unknown variable is...    nil
The player is at:
x:     50
y:     50
And its energy level is 100
```

If an error is displayed in the console, look at it carefully. You will see information about the kind of error and the position of the error in your code, expressed as a line number. Example:

```
Syntax error
.../main.lua:23: unexpected symbol near ')'
```

This means that the error is somewhere in line 23, and that something is wrong near the last parenthesis. Most of the time, the error is quite obvious.

```
23 print("The player is at:",)
```

Did you find the error? There is an unexpected comma before the second parenthesis. You'll learn some great tips and strategies for debugging your code in Part 5, but at this stage, being able to understand how to find and fix an error is enough.

Experiment by trying out your own variables and tracing their values, then head to the next chapter!

TO GO FURTHER . . .

You can read everything about variables, tables, and expressions in the official Lua documentation. Follow the link:

Types and values:

www.lua.org/pil/2.html

Tables:

www.lua.org/pil/2.5.html

Expressions:

www.lua.org/pil/3.html

Functions

Functions are ways to group instructions. A function can carry out a task, or it can compute something and return a result. A function can also receive parameters. These parameters are variables, and can be used in the function body.

What Does a Function Look Like?

Here is an example of a function:

```
Shot = function ()
        Energy = Energy - 10
End
```

A function can also be expressed as:

```
Function Shot()
        Energy = Energy - 10
End
```

The above two examples are of the same code, with two different syntaxes. The first version is the legacy way, and demonstrates that a function is like any other value. The second is a syntax shortcut.

I prefer the second example. Why? Because most programming languages use this kind of syntax, and it's easier to remember. I use this syntax in this book, but you can use either one.

A Function as a Task

This kind of function is autonomous. Let's say it's just performing a task, and that's it. For example, imagine that we need to reset several variables when a game session starts:

```
Function ResetGame()
        Score = 0
        Level = 1
        Energy = 100
End
```

The variables *Score*, *Level*, and *Energy* exist outside of the function and are modified by the function. The function will then be "called" like this:

```
-- Reset the game variables
ResetGame()
```

Functions Getting Parameters and Returning a Value

Sometimes you need to calculate something quite often. In this case, it's better (and cleaner) to group the instructions for the calculation in a function, and then return the result.

In most cases, you'll need to provide "parameters" for your function. It's like you're giving the cook the ingredients to a recipe, and asking the cook for the meal in return.

> **EXAMPLE:** Calculating the distance between two points is something we would need quite often, and the calculation is "indigestible," complex and not easy to read.

This function will receive two objects as parameters. These parameters are two tables. Each of these tables provides two variables: x and y.

At this stage, you don't have to pay attention to the calculation itself, just to the function structure. (I'm not a math whiz. I can find most of my answers using Google, and I still don't pay attention to the calculation . . . shh, don't tell anyone!)

Here is the code:

```
function getDistance(object1, object2)
      distance = math.sqrt(
            (object2.x-object1.x)^2+
            (object2.y-object1.y)^2)
      return distance
end
```

> **NOTE:** In Lua, you can cut a line of code into chunks if needed, like I did in this example. Just insert a few blank lines.

Look at the function call and how it receives the parameters. Now, here's how to call the function in your games:

```
foeDistance = getDistance(hero,foe)
print(foeDistance)
```

That's it. It's clean and readable, and you can call *getDistance* any time you need.

Functions in a Table

You can store a function in a variable. Let's enhance our *Energy* variable with a function to decrease it:

```
Energy = {}
Energy.level = 100
function Energy.Decrease(p)
      Energy.level = Energy.level - p
end

Energy.Decrease(10)
print(Energy.level)
```

Experiment

Create a new project with Corona Simulator called "TestFunctions" and type this code:

```
-- Your code here

function getDistance(object1, object2)
        distance = math.sqrt(
               (object2.x-object1.x)^2+
               (object2.y-object1.y)^2)
        return distance
end
```

```
object1 = {}
object1.x = 50
object1.y = 50

object2 = {}
object2.x = 100
object2.y = 100

dist = getDistance(object1, object2)

print("The distance is", dist)
```

The console should return this text:

```
The distance is 70.710678118655
```

Now experiment with creating more functions!

TO GO FURTHER . . .

You can read everything about Lua functions in the official Lua documentation here:

www.lua.org/pil/5.html

Control Structure Statements

What are control structure statements? Let's remember our "shopping list" metaphor: a list of instructions to your spouse.

These statements are the real intelligence of your code.

I don't want to put pressure on you . . . but you have to master this.

Conditional Statements

This is the basic control statement, and the most used: *If . . . Then . . . Else.*

With this amazing "if" statement, you're able to execute some code only if a certain condition is verified. I always use this example:

If it rains, take an umbrella.

In Lua and in a "game coding" situation, it looks like this:

```
if getDistance(hero, foe) < 100 then
      print "Alert"
end
```

This means that if the distance between the hero and the foe is less than 100, the trace "Alert" is displayed.

Here is the same example with an "else" statement added, and more than one line of code:

```
if getDistance(hero, foe) < 100 then
      print("Alert")
else
      print("Clear")
end
```

Pretty self-explanatory, right?

If you need several "if" statements in a row, use "elseif":

```
if energy < 10 then
      print("Red light")
elseif energy < 50 then
      print("Orange light")
else
      -- Default behavior
      print("Green light")
end
```

TOP TIP: Always read back your conditional statements, especially nested ones, and "execute" them in your mind, with different values as examples. You'll avoid many sneaky bugs.

Loop Statements

For

Let's start with my favorite: **For**.

The "for" loop is used to repeat a group of statements (lines of code) a specified number of times.

The "for" loop increases (or decreases) a variable at each step.

Here is an example:

```
for count=1,10 do
       print(count)
end
```

This small code will display 1 . . . 2 . . . 3 . . . 4 . . . until 10. The first parameter (1) is the start value, and the second parameter (10) is the end value. By default, the step value is 1.

Let's assume we need to display 10 . . . 9 . . . 8 . . . until 0:

```
for count=10,0,-1 do
       print(count)
end
```

In this example, count is decremented by 1 at each step (the third parameter is then the "step" value).

While

The second loop statement you'll have to use is "while." It will repeat a group of statements (lines of code) until a condition becomes true. It's quite simple to use. Here is an example:

```
while EnemyNumbers < 10
       AddEnemy()
       EnemyNumbers = EnemyNumbers + 1
end
```

In this example, the function "AddEnemy" will be called until *Enemy-Numbers* reaches 10.

> **TOP TIP:** The "while" statement is dangerous. It may cause infinite loops! In the last example, if we forgot to increment *EnemyNumbers*, the condition "< 10" will be true forever and your game will freeze.

Escape From a Loop!

If for any reason you need to jump out, use the "break" statement. Here is another clever example:

```
-- Jump out the loop when we found the right line
for count=1,10 do
        if hero.line == count then
                break
        end
end
```

Variable Scope: Local or Global?

Now we know what functions and statements are, we can talk about variable scope.

Global Scope

A global variable exists in your code and can be used right after being declared. For example, the variable *global_variable* declared in main.lua:

```
global_variable = "hello"
```

You can then use and modify *global_variable* anywhere in your code, including other Lua files.

It's great to use global variables, but it's dirty too . . . The main reason is the readability and reliability of your code. Using too many global variables will lead to bugs and hassles like "Where was this initialized?", "Where was this variable modified?", or "I'm bored! I'm going to bed right now!"

This is why local variables were invented.

Local Scope

A local variable is known only in the block where it is declared. A block is a statement (most of the time ending with "end"), a function, or a Lua file. To declare a variable or a function as local, just add *local* before its name:

```
local x = 100
```

Here is an illustration:

```
if energy <= 100 then
      local message = "Warning!"
      print(message)
end
-- at this stage, message is nil!
print(message)
```

If you type and execute this example, you'll find message to be nil (or undeclared) outside of the control statement "if *energy* . . ."

> **TIP:** Use a local variable anytime you know that the variable won't be used later in your code. It will avoid cluttering the memory with unused values or creating unexpected side effects, such as accidentally using a global variable initialized somewhere else in your code!

> **TOP TIP:** If you declare a global variable, it's great to use uppercase names. This makes your code highly readable, and enables you to guess which variable is global. Example: DEFAULT_ENERGY = 1000. It's great, as well, to declare global variables at the top of your Lua files, so you can easily find where they are initialized.

Experiment

Write a simple "for" loop, increasing a counter from 1 to 100. Then, in this loop, use an "if" statement to display (then "print" the result):

- "I'm a kid" if the counter is less than 15
- "I'm young" if the counter is between 30 and 59
- "I'm wise" if the counter is between 60 and 79
- "I ask for respect" for values between 80 and 100

TO GO FURTHER . . .

There is another loop statement called "repeat . . . until," but you won't have any difficulty understanding how it works. The "while" statement is more readable from my point of view.

You can read everything about Lua control structures in the official Lua documentation. Follow the link:

www.lua.org/pil/4.3.html

Arrays and Lists

In your games, you'll have to deal with a bunch of items, bullets, enemies, obstacles, and so forth. To store this kind of data in memory, you will use **arrays** or **lists**. You'll use an array when the number of items is known. Some examples are months, fixed gameplay elements, and inventory items. You'll use a list when the number of items is unknown and fluctuating (e.g., bullets, flying saucers, and other funny things a video game contains).

Arrays

Create an Array

In Lua, an array is nothing more than a table (see the chapter "Variables, Tables, and Expressions").

```
myShips = {}
```

Then, in the table, we insert data indexed with an integer like this:

```
myShips[1] = "Alpha"
myShips[2] = "Omega"
myShips[3] = "Delta"
```

An array element can be anything you need! Look at this:

```
myShips[1] = {}
myShips[1].name = "Alpha"
myShips[1].shield = 400
```

This is amazingly simple. You code like you think!
Another way to create an array "on the fly":

```
myShips = { "Alpha", "Omega", "Delta" }
```

An array element can even be an array itself. This is what we call a multidimensional array.

Browse an Array

Now we need to go through our array. You learned the "for" loop few pages earlier, so . . . Just iterate with an integer like this:

```
for i=1,3 do
      print(myShips[i])
end
```

This code will display the 3 ships' names in the console.

A better approach should be to iterate on the real size of the array. You can get the size of an array by adding # to the name of the array:

```
size = #myShips
```

So, here is the optimized code to browse the array:

```
for i=1,#myShips do
      print(myShips[i])
end
```

If you try to access an element outside of the array, you'll get **nil** as the value.

Lists

Create a List

A list is an array, but I prefer to explain the concept separately because if you have used another programming language, you may be used to seeing the both concepts as different.

With Lua, just consider a list as an advanced approach to creating arrays. With a list you can insert and remove items in an arbitrary order.

```
myList = {}
```

To populate a list, you'll use:

```
table.insert(myList, myElement)
```

The element names "myElement" in this example can be anything you need. It is added at the end of the list. To add an element to the beginning, just add the position as the first parameter :

```
table.insert(myList, 1, myElement)
```

Here is an example that creates 10 elements and stores them in a list:

```
myStarList = {}
for i=1,10 do
        local myStar = {}
        myStar.index = i
        table.insert(myStarList, myStar)
end
```

Browse a List

It's not the easy part. There are several ways to browse a list. Let me show you a generic way (the one I use in my games and apps).

```
for i in pairs(myStarList) do
        print(myStarList[i].index)
end
```

It is, from my point of view, the most readable way to browse a list.

Remove From a List

The table.remove function removes and returns an element from a list. It takes two arguments: the table and the position of the element. Here is how to remove the first element of *myStarList*:

```
table.remove(myStarList, 1)
```

> NOTE: I said that table.remove returns the element. Why? Because removing an element from a list does not remove it from memory. For example, if the element is a display object, you'll need to remove it from the list, then from the screen!

Experiment

Type and execute this code. Observe the behavior of the array and try to add and remove items of your own.

```lua
myShips = {}

myShips[1] = "Alpha"
myShips[2] = "Omega"
myShips[3] = "Delta"

print("Here is a simple array",#myShips)
for i=1,#myShips do
      print(i,myShips[i])
end

table.insert(myShips, 1, "Added first!")
table.insert(myShips, "Added last!")

print("Now it's a list!",#myShips)
for i=1,#myShips do
      print(i,myShips[i])
end

-- remove Alpha
table.remove(myShips, 2)

print("Alpha was destroyed",#myShips)
for i=1,#myShips do
      print(i,myShips[i])
end
```

TO GO FURTHER . . .

You can read everything about Lua tables as arrays and lists here:

http://lua-users.org/wiki/TablesTutorial

Object-Oriented
Programming With Lua

Some of you are already aware of what programmers call **OOP** (Object-Oriented Programming). Some of you may know nothing about it. I'll try to be as clear as I can here, to keep this simple for both groups.

First of all, I suggest you take a look at the Wikipedia page about OOP:

http://en.wikipedia.org/wiki/Object-oriented_programming

An object is a special type of variable bringing with it its properties (called fields) and its functions (called methods). We call this a "class." It allows you to organize your code to create "objects" of the same behaviors, like ships, characters, robots, and so on.

The academic metaphor is the vehicle:

- A vehicle has properties: color, weight, and so on.
- A vehicle has methods: go ahead, go back, break, and so on.

In a video game world, the academic example is the ship, or the alien!

Every time that you need to create several elements in your games that share the same behaviors and properties, you should think: "object!"

Is Lua an Object-Oriented Language?

Yes and no. It's not, but it can be.

Since I'm a professional Corona SDK programmer, I spent many hours browsing the web and experimenting with various ways to create objects with Lua. In the end, I found a way—a very simple way—that is used by many programmers. This is the way I'm going to teach you here.

> **WARNING:** The goal here is not to make you a Lua expert, but rather a game programmer. So I'll use some special features of Lua here without explaining them in great detail. The bottom line is that you'll still be able to create and use objects in your game.

The Simpler the Better

I'll give you a very simple sample: a "ship" class with only one property and one method, inspired by the ships of the previous chapter. You'll then be able to copy this class to create your own.

The Generic Class Sample

Here is a generic sample for a Lua class:

Class name: ***OOShip***
Property: ***Name,*** a string containing the name of the ship
Method: ***PrintName,*** a simple function displaying the name of the
 ship in the console

This can be reused and adapted according to your needs. To use this in your code, you just have to rename it and add your properties and functions:

File: ship.lua, it contains the class OOShip

```lua
OOShip = {}
local mt = {__index = OOShip}

-- Note the use of '.'
function OOShip.new(pName)
      local new_instance = {}
      new_instance.name = pName
      return setmetatable(new_instance,mt)
end

-- Note the use of ':'
function OOShip:PrintName()
      print(self.name)
end

return OOShip
```

To create a Ship object in your code, you just need few lines of code:

File: main.lua (or any other Lua file from your game)

```lua
ship = require("OOShip")

-- Create 2 different instances of ships
local ship1 = ship.new("alpha")
local ship2 = ship.new("beta")
```

```
ship1:PrintName()
ship2:PrintName()
```

Some Explanations

The first line is creating an empty table called OOShip (for Object-Oriented Ship):

```
OOShip = {}
```

The next line is preparing a special table, with an entry called __index, which is an internal Lua field:

```
local mt = {__index = OOShip}
```

We'll use this table in the constructor to be able to simulate OOP.

The following function is what we call the constructor. It creates the instance of the object, and prepares its default properties (also known as "fields"). In this example there is only one property, a string, called "name." Then, at the very end, it returns a "metatable" which is, in fact, the object instance.

Please note that the function name is preceded by the class name "OOShip" and a dot. We learned this before (see the chapter on *Functions*). It means that the function is a part of the table OOShip:

```
function OOShip.new(pName)
       local new_instance = {}
       new_instance.name = pName
       return setmetatable(new_instance,mt)
end
```

Then, we found the method PrintName of the object:

```
function OOShip:PrintName()
       print(self.name)
end
```

Please note the use of the colon (:) instead of the period (.)! It's a special way to declare a function in Lua. It means that the function will receive a special and hidden parameter called *self*. This *self* parameter will contain the instance of the object (with its attached properties and functions). Using the colon is a shortcut to avoid passing/receiving the self parameter.

Here, the function is using the traditional period:

```lua
function OOShip.PrintName(self)
      print(self.name)
end
```

It's the same function, but you can see the hidden parameter.

Experiment

Use the OOShip class sample to create a Hero class. Add 2 properties, x and y, as its coordinates. Then, add a method "MoveTo" receiving two parameters, px and py, and replace its coordinates with the received one.

Here's how your player class *Hero.lua* should look:

```lua
Hero = {}
local mt = {__index = Hero}

function Hero.new(px, py)
      local new_instance = {}
      new_instance.x = px
      new_instance.y = py
      return setmetatable(new_instance,mt)
end

function Hero:MoveTo(px,py)
      self.x = px
      self.y = py
end

return Hero
```

And a *main.lua* example using it:

```lua
hero = require("Hero")

local myHero = hero.new(10,10)
```

```
myHero:MoveTo(50,50)

print("myHero coordinates are",myHero.x,myHero.y)
```

TO GO FURTHER . . .

Here are some official links for Object-Oriented Programming with Lua:

http://lua-users.org/wiki/TablesTutorial

http://lua-users.org/wiki/MetamethodsTutorial

However, in this chapter you already have the most you'll ever need to create a game using some OOP!

Part 2
Display

Introduction

How was your journey in the Lua world? I'm sure you did not understand everything, and it's normal. One of my suggestions is to learn the basics and then practice, looking back at the previous lesson when needed.

In this part you'll start to use your knowledge (Lua programming) to display text, shapes, and images. In other words, to give life to your code!

The Screen Coordinate System

You have to know something very simple and important: the screen of your computer (and of your phone) is made with pixels. A pixel is a square dot. The number of pixels the screen can display horizontally and vertically is called the screen's **resolution.**

When you display something on the screen, you have to display it at a **coordinate.** A coordinate is expressed using its **horizontal and vertical position**. Commonly the horizontal coordinate is named **x** and the vertical coordinate is named **y**. The coordinate **0,0** means the first pixel at the **top left** of your screen.

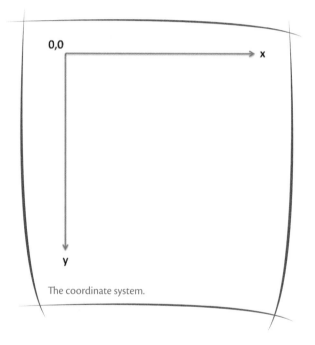

The coordinate system.

Display Objects

To display something you will create **display objects**. Anything that appears on your screen is a display object: a shape, an image, a button, and so forth.

Common Display Properties

There are several common values you'll need to display something. These are mainly related to the resolution of your screen. For example:

display.contentHeight

This is the number of pixels your game is able to display vertically.

display.contentWidth

This is the number of pixels your game is able to display horizontally.

display.contentCenterX

This is the horizontal position of the center of your screen. It's equivalent to display.contentWidth divided by 2.

display.contentCenterY

This is the vertical position of the center of your screen. It's equivalent to display.contentHeight divided by 2.

Take a look at this page to have an overview of the properties provided by Corona SDK regarding the screen:

http://docs.coronalabs.com/api/library/display/index.html

We'll dig into the screen system in the chapter "The Screen Jungles," but for now, the basics are quite enough!

Texts

Hey! You're going to display your first object on the device screen: a **text**!

Display a Simple Text

You can display a text anywhere on the screen with a single line of code:

```
display.newText("I was here. . .",
     100, 200, native.systemFont, 20)
```

This line of code creates a text object at the position 100 (x) and 200 (y) using the system font, with a height of 20 pixels.

Regarding the Position

The x and y positions refer to the center position of the text. If you need to position your object relative to its left, top, bottom, or right points, you need to modify the anchors before creating the text object.

Anchor points are used to align display objects around a particular relative point, and are specified in values between 0 and 1 where 0.5 is the center.

Here is how to display a text object on the left of the screen:

```
display.setDefault("anchorX", 0)
display.newText("I'm on the left. . .", 0, 50,
native.systemFont, 20)
display.setDefault("anchorX", 0.5)
```

Note that we need to revert the anchor back to its default behavior (center) after the text is created. Otherwise, the objects created afterwards will be left aligned, which is not the default behavior.

Regarding Fonts

There are two variants of the system font:

- native.systemFont
- native.systemFontBold

You can use custom fonts or use the available fonts on the device. It's out of our scope, but take a look at "To Go Further . . ." below for some tips.

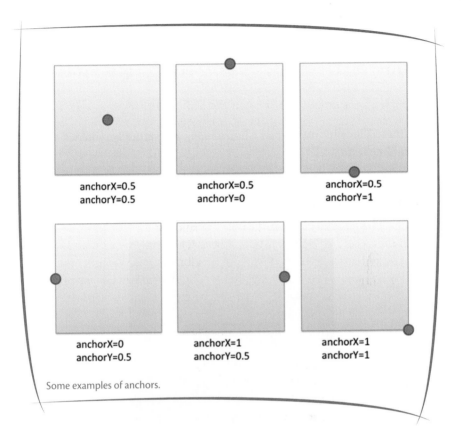

Some examples of anchors.

Display Multiline Text

If you need to display multiline text and align it, you must use advanced syntax. This syntax uses a table to combine the parameters:

```
options =
{
    text = "Hello world! This is my first
multiline text. Made with Corona SDK. . .",
    x = display.contentCenterX,
    y = display.contentCenterY,
    width = 300,
```

```
        font = native.systemFont,
        align = "center",
        fontSize = 25
}

local mytitle = display.newText(options)
```

These 2 lines of code display a horizontally and vertically centered multiline text.

Your first multiline text displayed centered!

The *align* property is only available with the advanced syntax and supports the following values : *left* (default), *right*, or *center*.

Practice

Experiment with the different behaviors of the text objects. Try to align texts on the right, on the left, or even on the bottom of the screen using anchorY and the display.contentHeight property.

TO GO FURTHER . . .

If you want to use custom fonts, I recommend this official FAQ:

http://coronalabs.com/blog/2013/01/16/faq-wednesday-custom-fonts/

For anchor points, refer to this official guide:

http://docs.coronalabs.com/guide/graphics/transform-anchor.html

Images

Now we're ready to draw basic shapes. We're going to learn how to display images like backgrounds, grounds, and crates. Then we'll create and display sprites.

An **image** is a picture, and most of the time contained in a file called a jpeg or a png. A **sprite** is one or several animated sequences of images. It is used in video games to display characters, animations, and so on. The main advantage of sprites is that all the images can be gathered in one big picture called the image sheet. There's a lot to learn here, but it's fun!

What Is an Image?

At the beginning of this chapter, I mentioned jpeg and png. How are they different? You just have to remember this:

- a **jpeg** is a rectangular picture, with no transparent parts.
- a **png** is a picture with transparent parts, so it allows nonrectangular images.

> PRO TIP: While jpeg files tend to be lighter than png, I always use jpeg when I don't need transparent parts in the asset.

Standard Image

A standard image is displayed using a single line of code:

```
local myImage = display.newImage("chicken.png")
```

It's important to understand that once the image has been displayed, it will remain on the screen forever until you remove it. It's a display object, and this is how Corona SDK deals with those. In some other low-level programming languages, we have to redraw the image over and over again on every frame. Thankfully, that's not the case with Corona SDK. Good news, right?

Dynamic Images

Standard Image and Device Resolution

A standard image (created with *newImage*) will not have the same rendering depending on which device it is displayed on. For example, the image will be crisp on an iPad with Retina display, but just so-so on an old iPhone 4. You'll say to yourself, why not provide only high-definition images? Because you will force Corona to scale down the image on low-resolution screens, causing bad performance and useless video memory consumption.

Bad, isn't it? But here comes Corona SDK! You can let Corona SDK deal with the image resolution, on one condition: you provide the images in both standard and high-definition resolutions.

Here is a dynamic image:

```
local myImageDynamic =
        display.newImageRect("chicken.png",
132, 153)
```

Here we used "display.newImageRect" which uses 2 additional parameters: the width and the height of the image.

Corona SDK will then compare the actual device size with the reference size of your app (set in the config.lua file), and select the image version that most closely matches the content area and scale. I suggest that you provide at least two versions of your images: one with standard resolution, and one with high-definition resolution.

To set up this dynamic image selection, you must:

1) Include an imageSuffix table within the content table of the *config. lua* file:

```
application = {
        content = {
                width = 320*2,
                height = 480*2,
                scale = "letterBox",
                fps = 30,

           imageSuffix = {
                ["@2x"] = 2,
                }
        },
}
```

2) Provide 2 files per image: the standard and the high-definition version. The high-definition image will be named with the "@2x" suffix as specified in the config.lua:

Standard: chicken.png
High-definition: chicken@2x.png

One of these chickens looks crispy . . .

It's a lot to digest, I know, but you have to master this part to be able to create apps that render best on devices of all sizes.

I will teach you everything in detail in the chapter "The Screen Jungles." Keep cool until then; you have more to learn.

TO GO FURTHER . . .

You can find everything about standard images objects here:
http://docs.coronalabs.com/api/library/display/newImage.html

And regarding dynamic images with imageRect:
http://docs.coronalabs.com/api/library/display/newImageRect.html

But do not forget to look at the project configuration guide:
http://docs.coronalabs.com/guide/basics/configSettings/index.html

Shapes

Shapes? Let's start with circles, lines, and rectangles.

Not so good at creating your own graphics? Using circles, lines, and rectangles is a smart and easy way to start a project without any graphics assets. You can also use circles, lines, and rectangles in your games to create great user interfaces or visual effects.

Circle

```
local head = display.newCircle(160, 100, 50)
```

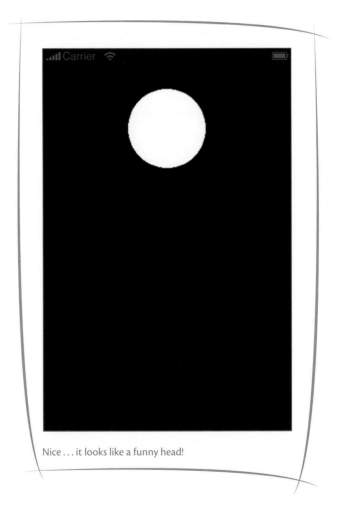

Nice . . . it looks like a funny head!

We'll color its face now. Add this line of code:

```
head:setFillColor(233/255, 205/255, 176/255)
```

Rectangle

To illustrate a rectangle, let's add a chest to the head:

```
local chest = display.newRect(160, 225, 50, 150)
chest:setFillColor(50/255, 200/255, 50/255)
```

Here is a nice chest . . . for a stick figure wearing an ugly green shirt. I like it!

Lines

We'll use lines to add some arms to our stick figure:

```
local arm1 = display.newLine(135, 160, 90, 290)
local arm2 = display.newLine(185, 160, 230, 290)
```

How does it look?
Hmm . . . The arms look a little thin . . . So, please add this:

```
arm1.strokeWidth = 10
arm2.strokeWidth = 10
```

And now . . . the legs:

```
local leg1 = display.newLine(140, 290, 140, 450)
local leg2 = display.newLine(180, 290, 180, 450)
```

It's done!

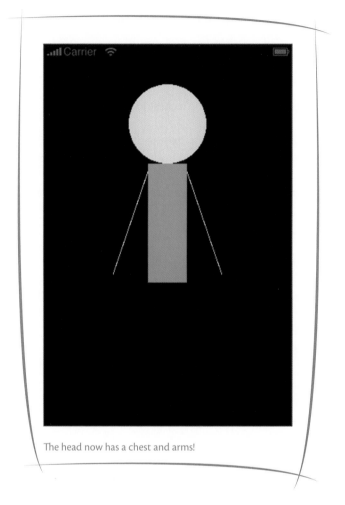

The head now has a chest and arms!

Combine Shapes and Text to Create Nice Interfaces

The examples below demonstrate a few clever ways to enhance text by using shapes to add a background, underline, or square.

A Title With a Background

We'll just draw a rectangle across the entire width, and draw the label on it. The result is a nice professional-looking title.

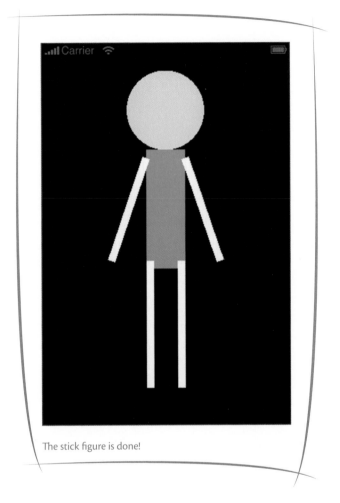

The stick figure is done!

```
-- Create a background rectangle for the title
local titleBackground =
    display.newRect(
        display.contentCenterX,
        50,
        display.actualContentWidth,
        50)
titleBackground:setFillColor(.2, .2, .4)
```

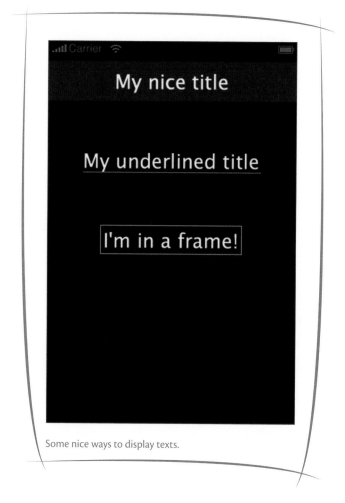

Some nice ways to display texts.

```
-- Create the label for the title at the same
position
options =
{
        text = "My nice title",
        x = display.contentCenterX,
        y = titleBackground.y,
        font = native.systemFont,
        fontSize = 25
}
local mytitle = display.newText(options)
```

An Underlined Title

Draw a label, then add a line between it. Simple!

```
-- An underlined title
options =
{
     text = "My underlined title",
     x = display.contentCenterX,
     y = 150,
     font = native.systemFont,
     fontSize = 25
}
local myTitle2 = display.newText(options)

-- Calculate the position and length of the
underline
local title2X1 = myTitle2.x - myTitle2.width/2
local title2X2 = myTitle2.x + myTitle2.width/2
local title2Y = myTitle2.y + myTitle2.height / 2
local title2Line = display.newLine(
     title2X1, title2Y, title2X2, title2Y)
title2Line:setStrokeColor(1, .3, .3)
```

A Squared Title

The classic squared label using just few lines of code!

```
-- A squared title
options =
{
     text = "I'm in a frame!",
     x = display.contentCenterX,
     y = 250,
     font = native.systemFont,
     fontSize = 25
}
local myTitle3 = display.newText(options)
```

```
-- The square
local padding = 5
local title3Square = display.newRect(
      myTitle3.x, myTitle3.y,
      myTitle3.width + padding, myTitle3.height
+ padding)
-- To be a square, the rect needs a stroke and a
transparent fill
title3Square.strokeWidth = 1
title3Square:setFillColor(0, 0)
title3Square:setStrokeColor(.6, .6, .8)
```

TO GO FURTHER . . .

You can find everything about shape objects in the official Shapes guide from Corona Labs:

http://docs.coronalabs.com/guide/graphics/path.html

Regarding the text object, look at the newtext API documentation:

http://docs.coronalabs.com/api/library/display/newText.html

Part 3
Move

Move Objects Around the Screen

Now that you're able to display some images and shapes, what about adding some movement?

While there is a simple way to move objects automatically using Corona SDK **transitions**, it would be great to be able to move the objects relative to user events like touches on the screen. For this purpose we'll introduce a new concept here: **events**.

Using Transitions to Move and Animate Objects

Transitions are a powerful way to move and animate objects over the screen. Transitions enable us to animate a display object numeric property from one value to another, in a determined time period. It's also defined as **interpolation**.

From Point to Point

To move an object from one point to another, the simplest way is to animate **x** and/or **y** with a transition. Let's look at this code:

```
local ball = display.newCircle(20, 20, 10)

transition.to(ball, { x=300, y=400, time=4000 })
```

In this example we created a 10-pixel radius circle (called *ball*) in the upper left corner of the screen (20,20), and then we asked Corona SDK to move it to the bottom right of the screen (300,400) in 4000 milliseconds.

Simple!

About the Parameters

```
transition.to(target, params)
```

Transitions methods receive a *target* (a display object) as the first parameter then a table *params* providing some attributes to describe the transition you want to start. The main attributes are the properties you want to animate with their final values (x=300, y=400) and the duration (time=4000).

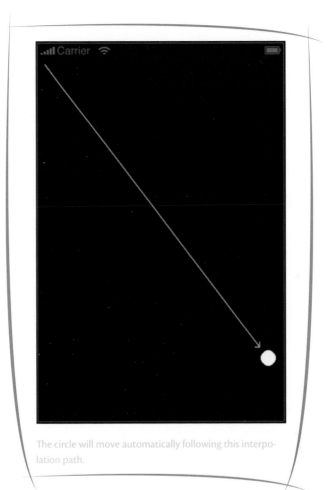

The circle will move automatically following this interpolation path.

Reverse Transition

In our first example, we moved our ball from its current position to another one. We can also do the opposite and move our ball from one position to the current one. Here is how:

```
local ball = display.newCircle(20, 20, 10)

transition.from(ball, { x=300, y=400, time=4000 })
```

Animate More Than the Position

It's great to be able to move an object, but what about animating its transparency, its rotation, or its scaling?

The transparency of a display object is determined by its *alpha* property, in which 1 is considered nontransparent and 0 is fully transparent. Let's animate the transparency of a rectangle to make it appear nicely on the screen:

```
local box = display.newRect(160, 200, 50, 50)

transition.from(box, { alpha = 0, time=2000 })
```

As you can see, we animated the alpha from 0 to the current value, which is 1 by default. The other, less direct way to do this is with *transition.to*:

```
local box = display.newRect(160, 200, 50, 50)

box.alpha = 0

transition.to(box, { alpha = 1, time=2000 })
```

Now, let's add a rotation to the animation:

```
local box = display.newRect(160, 200, 50, 50)

transition.from(box, { alpha = 0, rotation = 180,
time=2000 })
```

As you can see, you're able to combine several animated properties! Any numeric property can be animated with transitions: *height, width, xScale, yScale, alpha* . . .

xScale and yScale represent the scale factor of a display object, where 1 is the original size. For example, if you change the xScale property of a display object to 2, it doubles its width.

Let's animate the xScale of a rectangle:

```
local box = display.newRect(160, 200, 50, 50)

transition.to(box, { xScale = 0.5, time=1000 })
```

Smooth Transitions

Now that we know how to animate some properties, let's add some fun.

In our example, the properties (x, y, rotation, alpha) were animated linearly. Adding an **easing method** to the transition allows us to add some nonlinear movements like bounce effect, acceleration, deceleration, and so forth. There are dozens of easing methods!

Here is an outExpo effect giving the illusion that the circle lands smoothly in its final position:

```
local ball = display.newCircle(100, 160, 10)

transition.to(ball, { x = 250, time=1000,
transition = easing.outExpo })
```

And to add a funny bounce effect, just change the transition to:

```
transition.to(ball, { x = 250, time=1000,
transition = easing.outBounce })
```

You can look at all 42 easing methods in the official documentation, each one with a nice drawing to illustrate the effect:

http://docs.coronalabs.com/api/library/easing/index.html

onComplete

A transition would not be so powerful without the ability to trigger a function when the transition is over. There are several ways to do this; here are my favorites:

- Chain transitions, like bounces back and forth
- Displaying something when a transition is over
- Playing a sound when a transition is over

Here is a bouncing example:

```
ball = display.newCircle(160, 100, 10)

function ballDown()
      transition.to(ball, { y = 200, time=1000,
            transition = easing.inQuad,
      onComplete = ballUp })
end

function ballUp(ball)
      transition.to(ball, { y = 100, time=1000,
            transition = easing.outQuad,
      onComplete = ballDown })
end

ballDown()
```

Read the code carefully. There are two functions, one of the falling ball, the other moving it back to its upper position. Each one is calling the other when the transition is over using *onComplete*. We then just have to create the ball and make it fall by calling *ballDown* once!

This other example displays a text (using a fade-in transition!) when a circle reaches its final position:

```
box = display.newRect(160, 20, 50, 50)

boxText = display.newText("I'm done!", 160, 440)

function boxDone()
      transition.to(boxText, { alpha = 1, time =
500 })
end

boxText.alpha = 0

transition.to(box, { y = 400, time = 2000,
      transition = easing.outExpo, onComplete =
boxDone })
```

You should be able to easily understand this last example. We create a box and a text, the text being invisible (*alpha* = 0); then we animate the box and call a function to display the text (smoothly!) when the transition is done.

> **TOP TIP:** With Lua you're able to declare the function on the fly, inside the transition call! Here is how:

```
transition.to(box,
      { y = 400, time = 2000, transition =
easing.outExpo,
            onComplete = function()
                  transition.to(boxText, { alpha
= 1, time = 500 })
            end
      })
```

Cancel and Pause Transitions

Once a transition has started, it's best to keep its reference to be able to cancel or pause it. For example, if the user moves to the menu of your game, or loses the game (GAME OVER!), you need to cancel the running transitions to avoid weird behavior or bugs.

Here is how to keep a transition reference to cancel it later:

Regarding Transition Tags

Corona SDK introduced transition tags to add the ability to cancel or pause a group of transitions sharing the same tag. Here is an example:

Convenient Methods

If you want, you can use some convenient methods provided by Corona SDK. Some of them are useless like moveTo or scaleTo, but the others allow you to focus on the effect, not the properties to animate.

Here are these methods, each one provided as an example:

```
transition.blink()
transition.dissolve()
```

```
transition.fadeIn()
transition.fadeOut()
transition.moveBy()
transition.moveTo()
transition.scaleBy()
transition.scaleTo()
```

Practice

Be sure to experiment with transitions to create some nice and fun effects. As another exercise, revisit the chapter on images and animate an image instead of circle and rectangles.

Do you remember the familiar game with a plumber jumping everywhere? Remember the rotating coins? Achieve this effect with what you have learned! Here are some clues:

- Animate the xScale back and forth.
- Use onComplete to chain xScale transitions.

Remember the game with the flapping bird? You can make the pipe move from right to left using a transition too. Let's do it!

TO GO FURTHER . . .

Here are some useful links from the official documentation:

First, the starting point, everything about the transition library:

http://docs.coronalabs.com/api/library/transition/index.html

Then, the reference guide for the easing functions, with visuals:

http://docs.coronalabs.com/api/library/easing/index.html

Move Objects Around the Screen

The Interactive Way

It's moving? Now let's add some interactivity with user inputs. This section will teach you how to move objects in response to taps and finger movements on the screen.

A user input can take various forms: a single tap, a tap followed by a move, or a device movement like a shake.

Each time the user interacts with the device, an **event** is sent to your code. To react to this event, you need to "catch" it. We can catch an event by "listening" to it with an **event listener**.

Listen to a Tap Event

The simplest way to get user input is by listening to the **tap** event. A tap event is sent when the user "taps" an object on the screen. No more, no less. It's great for "one shot" actions.

Here is a simple tap listener on a circle, which can represent a button:

```
local myBtn = display.newCircle(60, 420, 20)

function onBtn(event)
        print("Tap on Left")
end

myBtn:addEventListener("tap", onBtn)
```

What about adding a nice effect on the circle using our new transition expertise? Add this code in the OnBtn function:

```
transition.from(myBtn, {time=1000, xScale=.8,
yScale=.8, transition=easing.outElastic})
```

Got it? This single line of code will make our circle bounce when tapped!

Listen to a Touch Event

The advanced tap event is called **touch**. It occurs when the user touches an object on the screen, and it can be split into 3 phases:

1) The user touches the object: the "**began**" phase.
2) The user moves over the object: the "**moved**" phase.
3) The user removes their finger from the screen: the "**ended**" phase.

Let's repeat the 3 phases: **began . . . moved . . . ended**.
Try this code to illustrate the touch event:

```
local myObject = display.newRect(display.
contentCenterX,
        display.contentCenterY, 50, 50)

myObject:setFillColor(255)

function onTouch(event)
        print(event.phase)

        return true
end

myObject:addEventListener("touch", onTouch)
```

In these few lines of code, we:

- Created a 50x50 pixel square centered on the screen
- Filled it with white
- Declared a listener function called onTouch
- Added a "touch" listener to our app, attached to the square, and
  calling the onTouch function

Like the **tap** event, the onTouch function receives an automatic
parameter that we called **event** and provides some useful information
regarding the event, the most useful being the **phase**.

To get the phase inside the listener function, just use **event.phase**. As
you can see in this example, we just print the phase in the console. Try
to touch, move in and out . . . look at the console to be familiar with the
behavior of the touch event.

> **PRO TIP:** For cleaner code, you should attach your listener function
> to the display object itself. Here is how:

```
function myObject:touch(event)
        print(event.phase)

        return true
end

myObject:addEventListener("touch", myObject)
```

> **TIP:** Replacing "onTouch" with "myObject" in the addEventListener call will make Corona add a function to the object itself. This function takes the name of the event. In this example the event is "touch," so the function added to the display object is called "touch." This prevents you from having duplicate functions with similar names, and avoids bugs if you use the same name by mistake. It's not a big deal, but it's a bit like storing your functions in the right drawers!

Use the Touch Event to Drag an Object on the Screen

We're now almost ready to drag the square across the screen! But as you might have guessed, there is an issue with our previous example. When the finger swipes out of the square, no more **moved** phases from the touch event are sent to our square.

To enable the event to be sent, we'll ask Corona SDK to "focus" on our object while the touch event starts. For this purpose, we'll use the **setFocus** API.

The **setFocus** API needs to be applied on the root group of the object we want to focus on. It's like asking all the objects from the screen to forward any further events to the designated object.

Corona SDK provides a simple way to get this root group:

```
display.getCurrentStage()
```

Then we'll need to set a flag to **true** to know if the user is currently dragging the object or not. It's quite easy: we'll set this flag to true on the **began** phase, and set it to false on the **ended** phase. The rest of the time, if we get a **moved** on the object, we'll know if we need to drag it or not!

Here is the full code:

```
local myObject = display.newRect(display.
contentCenterX, display.contentCenterY, 50, 50)
myObject:setFillColor(255)

function myObject:touch(event)
    if event.phase == "began" then
        display.getCurrentStage():
```

```
            setFocus(self)
            self.isDrag = true

            self.initX = self.x
            self.initY = self.y

    elseif self.isDrag then
            if event.phase == "moved" then
                self.x = event.x - event.
                xStart + self.initX
                self.y = event.y - event.
                yStart + self.initY
            elseif event.phase == "ended" or
            event.phase == "cancelled" then
                display.getCurrentStage():
                setFocus(nil)
                self.isDrag = false
            end
    end

    return true
end

myObject:addEventListener("touch", myObject)
```

Amazing!

If you're not sure that you understand the purpose of the isDrag flag, try not to use it (comment the lines involving it with two hyphens: "--"), and then drag your finger (actually, from the Corona Simulator, the mouse with the left button pressed) from the outside of the square, and then move on it. The square gets some touch events (with "moved" phases) that it should ignore, and goes crazy!

> **PRO TIP:** To understand a code from another coder, the best way is to play with it by commenting on the parts that you don't understand the need for. Next, run the code and see what bugs result. Then, change some values and look at the impact. By doing it this way, you'll be more comfortable with the code.

Practice

I challenge you to combine these last two lessons. Let's add two circle buttons to the very last example (the "drag the square"). One of these circle buttons will make the square move to the left of the screen using a transition, and the other to the right.

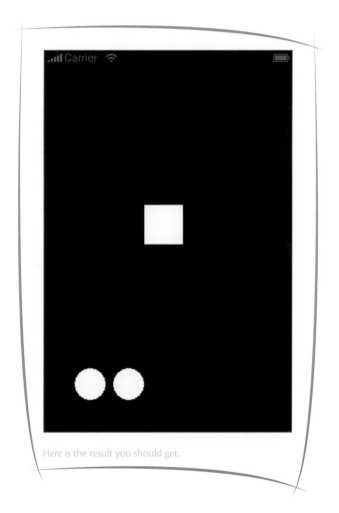

Here is the result you should get.

Ready? Go!

Move Objects Around the Screen

Frame by Frame

It's sometime necessary to move objects across the screen with full control. Transitions are great, but they aren't the answer for everything. I'll teach you how to perform a code of your own every time the system displays a frame on the screen. This will give you full control over movements on the screen.

Keep in mind, however, that performing a code 60 times per second is bad for the app's performance. So, any time you can use a simple event or a transition instead, your app will thank you.

What Is a Frame?

While it's not obvious when using an advanced SDK like Corona SDK, every system is refreshing its display many times per second—around 60! A refresh is called a **frame**. Perhaps you've seen the acronym FPS somewhere? It means frame per second, which is the "frame rate." Most game coders will target a 60 FPS frame rate for a perfectly smooth game.

Please note that you can get the current frame rate by calling *display. fps*; for example:

```
Print ("Current FPS", display.fps)
```

If you perform too many things in your code, or if your game displays a lot of moving objects at the same time, the frame rate can be impacted, and your game will slow down.

It's also important to know that Corona SDK apps run with a limit of 30 FPS by default. To change this, you need to add/modify a line in the file called **config.lua**. To run your app at 60 FPS, change the fps value to 60 by doing this:

```
application = {
    content = {
            width = 320,
            height = 480,
            scale = "letterBox",
            fps = 60,
    },
}
```

The EnterFrame Event

Every time a frame is about to be displayed, Corona SDK sends an "EnterFrame" event. Here is how to implement the EnterFrame event:

```
local myListener = function(event)
      print("A new frame!")
end

Runtime:addEventListener("enterFrame",
myListener)
```

Try this code to experiment, but with the exception of debugging purposes, do not print anything in the EnterFrame event to avoid your console to be filled with annoying traces!

Moving a Ball Every Frame

Let's move a ball across the screen using the EnterFrame event.

```
local ball = display.newCircle(display.
contentCenterX, display.contentCenterY, 20)
local xMove = 5
local yMove = 5
local myListener = function(event)
      ball.x = ball.x + xMove
      ball.y = ball.y + yMove

      if ball.x < 0 or ball.x > display.
contentWidth then
      xMove = 0 - xMove
end
if ball.y < 0 or ball.y > display.contentHeight
then
      yMove = 0 - yMove
      end
end
Runtime:addEventListener("enterFrame",
myListener)
```

Here it is! Here we just created a circle shape and we moved it around the screen by changing its x and y properties. By default, we increased both x and y, making the ball follow a diagonal. Then, when the ball reached an edge, we reversed the move.

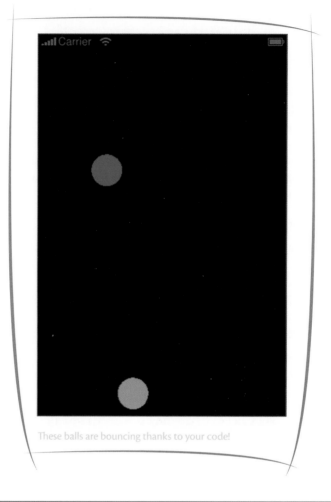

These balls are bouncing thanks to your code!

> **TIP:** To reverse a value, just change it from positive to negative, or vice versa. For example, if 0 − 1 = −1, then change it to 0 − (−1) = −1. This is useful for bouncing things.

Warning: It's Bad, But . . .

As I said earlier, it's a bad idea to perform too much code in the Enter-Frame event. Additionally, moving an object in the EnterFrame event will make the object move at different speeds depending on the device's performance, which is not the case with transitions (because transitions use time references).

You can resolve this issue by calculating the time elapsed since the last frame. (The value you'll get is called the "delta time," or "delta" by coding insiders). If the device runs slowly, this delta will be higher, so the trick is to multiply all the values you use to change positions with this delta:

```
local tPrevious = system.getTimer()
local myListener = function(event)
     local tDelta = (event.time - tPrevious) / 10
     tPrevious = event.time
     ball.x = ball.x + xMove * tDelta
     ball.y = ball.y + yMove * tDelta
     . . .
```

Practice

Here's a simple exercise: Add a third ball that moves only vertically, starting at the center of the screen.

Another one, tougher this time: Create a star field using the List lesson you just learned. Create a bunch of dots using a small circle, store them in a list, make them move from one side of the screen to another frame by frame, then translate the ones moving outside of the screen to the opposite!

TO GO FURTHER . . .

A tutorial about the EnterFrame event:
http://coronalabs.com/blog/2012/02/21/understanding-coronas-enterframe-event/

The EnterFrame event documentation:
http://docs.coronalabs.com/api/event/enterFrame/index.html

Make Them Fall

The Physics Engine

There's a smart way to deal with object movements, which is to let the engine do the job for you! If your game idea fits with it, the **physics engine** will do a lot of the heavy lifting.

The physics engine adds life to your game objects by giving them weight and consistency, which allows objects to fall, bounce, and collide. Games like Angry Birds are great examples of the physics engine doing its job.

A Bouncing Ball in 6 Lines of Code

```
physics = require("physics")
physics.start()

local ground = display.newRect(display.
    contentCenterX, 470, display.contentWidth,
    20)
physics.addBody(ground, "static")

local ball = display.newCircle(display.
contentCenterX, 0, 20)
physics.addBody(ball, "dynamic", {density=1,
bounce=0.4, radius=20})
```

Type this code into your editor, run it, and look at how the ball is falling and bouncing, where your code is not doing anything!

Let me explain the code:

1) We require a Corona component called "physics," then we start the physics engine.
2) We create a rectangle at the bottom of the screen.
3) We add a simple body to the rectangle. This body is "static," which means it won't fall! These kinds of bodies interact with others bodies but do not move.
4) We create a ball, with a radius of 20.
5) We're adding a "dynamic" and circle body to the ball with some density and bouncing characteristics. Adding "radius" to the body lets Corona know that the body is circular and not rectangular.

NOTE: Corona SDK uses the Box2D engine, which is one of the most popular in the game coding world. Thousands of games are implementing it. Corona SDK lets you use it with some degree of simplicity, but remember that this engine is huge (and very powerful too). I'm providing enough guidance here for you to get started.

Some Words Regarding addBody

Here is the simple syntax:

```
physics.addBody(object, [bodyType,] { density=d,
friction=f, bounce=b })
```

- *object* is the display object you want to add a body to. It can be a shape or an image.
- *bodyType* is a string describing the type of body. It can be "dynamic," "static," or "kinematic." The most common are dynamic, like the bouncing ball, and static, like the ground. Kinematic bodies are not influenced by gravity, but can move under simulation according to their velocity.
- *density* is part of the third parameter table. It describes the density of the object, knowing that water has a density of 1. Wood has a lower density, while metal has a higher density.
- *friction* influences how the object velocity will slow down when the object is moving.
- *bounce* describes how elastic the object is. This value will make the difference between a rubber ball (bounce=0.4, for example) and a metal ball (bounce=0).

There is another property to add to the third parameter table of addBody. This property will inform the engine about the shape of the object.

Rectangular Body

By default, the body is rectangular and the body boundaries will snap to the rectangular boundaries of the display object.

Circular Body

Just add *radius=r* to the table, where *r* is the radius of the object. This is the ball example.

Complex Body

Corona SDK allows bodies to have very complex shapes, even multi-art bodies, but it's beyond the scope of this book. That said, if your object has a nonrectangular and noncircular shape, the simplest way is to use the outline feature (which is limited to Pro and Enterprise Corona users). Here is an example:

```
local imageOutline = graphics.newOutline(2,
"myobject.png")
local image = display.newImage("myobject.png")
physics.addBody(image, { outline=imageOutline,
bounce=0.5 })
```

Practice: Create a Ball Fountain

To help you become a master of the physics engine, here's a nice sample that combines a lot of the knowledge you've learned in this book so far. The result is a fountain of balls bouncing on your phone screen! Nice . . .

Let's start the physics engine and display the bodies for debug (and understanding) using the hybrid mode of the engine:

```
physics = require("physics")
physics.setDrawMode("hybrid")

physics.start()
```

Then, let's create a function to create a new ball. We'll color it randomly and give it a small velocity so that not all the balls fall vertically. This will create a nice fountain effect:

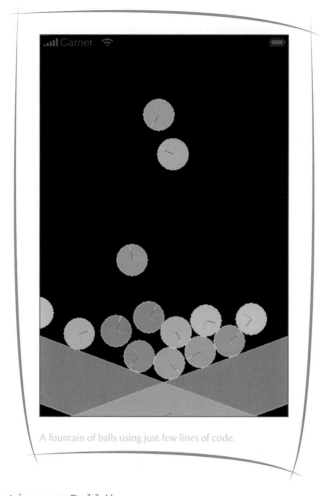

A fountain of balls using just few lines of code.

```
function newBall()
      local ball = display.newCircle(display.
contentCenterX+math.random(-10,10), 100, 20)
      ball:setFillColor(math.random(), math.
random(), math.random())
      ball.rotation = math.random(0,360)
      physics.addBody(ball, "dynamic", { radius
= 20, density=1.0, friction=0.3, bounce=0.5 })
      ball:setLinearVelocity(math.random
(-50,50), 0)
end
```

Now, the ground! Because I do not want the balls to fall out of the screen, we'll create two tilted and static grounds, to simulate a kind of pit:

```
local ground1 = display.newRect(display.
contentCenterX, display.contentHeight, display.
contentWidth*2, 80)
ground1.rotation = -20
physics.addBody(ground1, "static", {
density=1.0})
local ground2 = display.newRect(display.
contentCenterX, display.contentHeight, display.
contentWidth*2, 80)
ground2.rotation = 20
physics.addBody(ground2, "static", {
density=1.0})
ground1:setFillColor(.5, .1, .5)
ground2:setFillColor(.5, .1, .5)
```

And now, just create 20 balls, one every 500 milliseconds:

```
timer.performWithDelay(500, newBall, 20)
```

Enjoy!

> NOTE: Comment the physics.setDrawMode ("hybrid") line to see the sample without the debug shape displayed.

Adding Collision Detection

Every time two physics objects collide, a collision event is raised. We just have to listen to this event to detect collision:

```
local function onCollision(event)
        -- Your code here
end
```

```
Runtime:addEventListener("collision",
  onCollision)
```

Each collision event includes *event.object1* and *event.object2*, which contain the two Corona display objects involved in the collision. But it's not enough. We'll use a property called "myName" to know which object is colliding with another. It's not part of the physics engine; it's a custom property. We'll add a name to all the balls and to the ground. Here is how to do it for the first ground:

```
ground1.myName = "ground #1"
```

For the balls, we'll use a global counter called *ballNumber* to number the balls.

Here is the full code:

```
physics = require("physics")
physics.setDrawMode("hybrid")

physics.start()

local ballNumber = 0

function newBall()
      local ball = display.newCircle(display.
contentCenterX+math.random(-10,10), 100, 20)
      ball:setFillColor(math.random(), math.
random(), math.random())
      ball.rotation = math.random(0,360)
      physics.addBody(ball, "dynamic", { radius
= 20, density=1.0, friction=0.3, bounce=0.5 })
      ball:setLinearVelocity(math
random(-50,50), 0)
      ball.myName="ball #"..ballNumber
      ballNumber = ballNumber + 1
end
```

```
local ground1 = display.newRect(display.
contentCenterX, display.contentHeight, display.
contentWidth*2, 80)
ground1.rotation = -20
ground1.myName = "ground #1"
physics.addBody(ground1, "static", {
density=1.0})
local ground2 = display.newRect(display.
contentCenterX, display.contentHeight, display.
contentWidth*2, 80)
ground2.rotation = 20
ground2.myName = "ground #2"
physics.addBody(ground2, "static", {
density=1.0})
ground1:setFillColor(.5, .1, .5)
ground2:setFillColor(.5, .1, .5)

local function onCollision(event)
    if (event.phase == "began") then
        print("began collision between:
" .. event.object1.myName .. " and " .. event.
object2.myName)
    elseif (event.phase == "ended") then
        print("ended collision between:
" .. event.object1.myName .. " and " .. event.
object2.myName)
    end
end
Runtime:addEventListener("collision",
onCollision)

timer.performWithDelay(500, newBall, 20)
```

TO GO FURTHER . . .

Look deeply in the Corona SDK documentation and samples to master the physics engine. Here are some useful links.

Everything about physics bodies:

http://docs.coronalabs.com/guide/physics/physicsBodies/index.html

A tutorial to create physics bodies from image textures (outline):

http://coronalabs.com/blog/2014/01/28/tutorial-create-physics-bodies-from-texture-assets/

Make Them Collide
But Not Fall

A game is not a game if nothing collides, but not all games need physics! The physics engine offers the simplest way to deal with collisions; however, adding a body to an object makes it fall on the screen. Funny, but useless!

Using Physics Without Physics

In this lesson, we'll deactivate all the behaviors of physics to retain only the collision part. You have just 2 simple things to do to keep the collisions active but not the physics behavior:

1) Remove the effects of gravity:

```
physics.setGravity(0,0)
```

2) Use dynamic sensor bodies:

```
physics.addBody(ball1, "dynamic",
{ isSensor=true, radius = 20 })
```

Then we need to raise an event when a collision occurs:

```
local function onCollision(event)

    if (event.phase == "began") then

      print("Collision occurs")
    end
end

Runtime:addEventListener("collision",
onCollision)
```

What about using our FrameBall example to add collisions? Here is the updated sample:

```
physics = require("physics")

physics.start()
physics.setGravity(0,0)

local ball1 = display.newCircle(display.
contentCenterX, 100, 20)
ball1:setFillColor(math.random(), math.random(),
```

```
math.random())
physics.addBody(ball1, "dynamic",
{ isSensor=true, radius = 20 })
ball1.xMove = math.random(1,5)
ball1.yMove = math.random(1,5)

local ball2 = display.newCircle(display.
contentCenterX, 300, 20)
ball2:setFillColor(math.random(), math.random(),
math.random())
physics.addBody(ball2, "dynamic",
{ isSensor=true, radius = 20 })
ball2.xMove = math.random(1,5)
ball2.yMove = math.random(1,5)

local tPrevious = system.getTimer()
local myListener = function(event)
      local tDelta = (event.time - tPrevious) / 10
      tPrevious = event.time

      -- Keep the current ball positions safe
      local previousXball1 = ball1.x
      local previousYball1 = ball1.y
      local previousXball2 = ball2.x
      local previousYball2 = ball2.y

      ball1.x = ball1.x + (ball1.xMove * tDelta)
      ball1.y = ball1.y + (ball1.yMove * tDelta)
      ball2.x = ball2.x + (ball2.xMove * tDelta)
      ball2.y = ball2.y + (ball2.yMove * tDelta)

      -- if a ball reaches an edge,
      -- we reverse the motion and restore the
ball to its previous
      -- position on its axis

      if ball1.x <= 0 or ball1.x >= display.
contentWidth then
            ball1.xMove = 0 - ball1.xMove
```

```
                ball1.x = previousXball1
        end
        if ball1.y <= 0 or ball1.y >= display.
contentHeight then
                ball1.yMove = 0 - ball1.yMove
                ball1.y = previousYball1
        end
        if ball2.x <= 0 or ball2.x >= display.
contentWidth then
                ball2.xMove = 0 - ball2.xMove
                ball2.x = previousXball2
        end
        if ball2.y <= 0 or ball2.y >= display.
contentHeight then
                ball2.yMove = 0 - ball2.yMove
                ball2.y = previousYball2
        end
end

local function onCollision(event)
        if (event.phase == "began") then
          print("Collision occurs")
                event.object1:setFillColor(math.
random(), math.random(), math.random())
                event.object2:setFillColor(math.
random(), math.random(), math.random())
        end
end

Runtime:addEventListener("collision",
onCollision)
Runtime:addEventListener("enterFrame",
myListener)
```

As you can see, we are randomly changing the colors of the circles when they collide.

In this lesson, we managed to detect a collision between 2 graphical objects without using any strange code. Nice!

Which Objects Are Colliding?

In a game, it's very important to understand which objects are colliding: 2 bullets together, our ship and a wall, or a bullet and a head? As we saw in the previous chapter, Lua allows this with a simple line of code.

Because the images or shapes you're using are Lua tables, you can add arbitrary data to these tables. Just add these lines of code at the beginning, right after creating ball1 and ball2:

```
ball1.myName = "ball #1"
ball2.myName = "ball #2"
```

This data is now available in the collision event:

```
local function onCollision(event)

        if (event.phase == "began") then
            print("Collision occurs")
            print("Object 1=",event.object1.
myName)
            print("Object 2=",event.object2.
myName)
    ...
```

Now we can see, in the console, the names of our balls when they collide. This isn't very useful as there are only two objects on the screen. Let's add a wall. Input this code after the creation of the 2 balls:

```
local wall = display.newRect(display.
contentCenterX, display.contentCenterY, 100, 50)
wall.myName = "the wall..."
wall:setFillColor(math.random(), math.random(),
math.random())
physics.addBody(wall, "dynamic", { isSensor=true })
```

Compile, run . . . Tada!

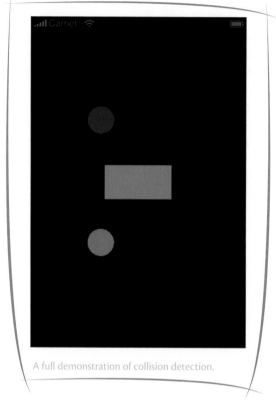

A full demonstration of collision detection.

Practice

You now have enough knowledge to create a basic Space Invaders–type game!

Create a basic game with:

- A ship at the bottom of the screen, with 3 buttons to move it from left to right and fire a bullet.
- Some aliens on the top (no need to make them move at this stage).
- Code (using the tap event) that assigns actions to the 3 buttons:

  - 1 left button: to decrease the x position of the ship
  - 1 right button: to increase the x position of the ship
  - 1 fire button: to create a bullet (can be a small circle) that moves from the ship position to the top of the screen using a transition (or frame by frame if you prefer)

- Adding a collision event to detect a collision between a bullet and an alien, making the alien disappear!

Ready? Go!

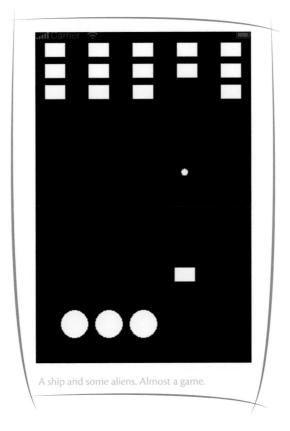

A ship and some aliens. Almost a game.

The full sample is available on the online book companion link.

TO GO FURTHER . . .

You can go deeper with collisions; this was just an introduction that covered the basics.

Here is an official guide regarding collision detection:

http://docs.coronalabs.com/guide/physics/collisionDetection/

Animate Images
With Sprites

A sprite is an image, usually animated, that is displayed on your screen. The term "sprite" is a legacy of the first computers and consoles, where it referred to a graphical object that a computer could display and move on the screen. For our part, sprites in Corona SDK offer a powerful way to store and animate game items like characters, bullets, balls, and other things.

> **KEY POINT:** Sprite images are stored in **image sheets**. An image sheet combines numerous small images into a larger image. It allows storing many images in one, creating frame-by-frame animations, and reducing processing time.

Image Sheets

To build an image sheet, you have two options:

1) Build the image by yourself, manually, using a tool like Photoshop or Gimp. It's not the easiest way, but I'll still explain it briefly.
2) Use a tool!

> **KEY POINT:** There are several tools available for building image sheets, so feel free to choose your favorite.
> My favorite is Texture Packer. It is available for Mac and Windows:
> www.codeandweb.com/texturepacker/coronasdk
> Consider paying for tools like these . . . they are definitely worth it!

Using a tool is fast and user friendly. It does a lot of the work for you, supports multiple sizes for the different resolutions, and arranges the images in the sheet to reduce its size. The bad news: these tools are not free. However, I would consider them must-haves.

Texture Packer is ideal because it supports both Windows and Mac. Zwoptex is great too, because it's very simple to use, and cheap, but at the time of writing it only runs on Mac.

Create an Image Sheet Manually

Creating an image sheet is simple when you need to combine images of the same size.

Using your image editor (Photoshop, Gimp, etc.), combine your images horizontally. In the following example, I have created an animation with 4 frames. My sprite is a chicken that is 174×160, so I need an image of height 160 and width 696 (174×4).

Save it as a png with transparency, and call the file "chicken_hand-made.png."

A sprite sheet made by hand!

From the code side it's quite simple, as you just have to describe the size of the sprite and the number of frames:

```
local options =
{
        width = 174,
        height = 160,
        numFrames = 4
}
```

```
local sheet_handmade = graphics.
newImageSheet("chicken_handmade.png", options)
```

Create an Image Sheet With Texture Packer

1) Create a folder containing the images of your sprites.
2) Download and launch Texture Packer.
3) Drop your folder in Texture Packer.
4) Choose "Corona SDK (image sheet)" in the Data Format drop-down box.
5) Click on Publish and name your sheet "chicken_packer" for the example.
6) You're done!

Our sprite sheet with Texture Packer.

Now, here is the code to use the generated image sheet in your code:

```
local sheetInfo = require("chicken_packer")
local spriteSheet = graphics.
newImageSheet("chicken_packer.png",
sheetInfo:getSheet())
```

Display and Animate Sprites

Because sprites are made to be animated, you need to describe animated sequences in order to display your sprites. In our example, the animation is made with 4 frames.

If you made your sprite sheet without any tool, you're sure to have your frames in a sequential order. Here is how to create the sequence and display the sprite.

1) Load the sprite sheet (see above).
2) Describe an animation and create the sprite:

```
local sequenceData1 =
{
    name="fly",
    start=1,
    count=4,
    time=250,
    loopCount = 0,
    loopDirection = "bounce"
}

local chicken1 = display.newSprite(sheet_
handmade, sequenceData1)
```

Some notes regarding the option table:

- This animation is called "fly" (*name*). In a game, some characters can use several animations: jump, run, explode, and so forth.
- The animation starts with the first frame (*start*), and is composed of 4 frames (*count*).
- Each frame is displayed for 250 milliseconds (*time*).

- The animation loops indefinitely (*loop*=0).
- The animation bounce (*loopDirection*) means that the animation will play forward then backward through the sequence of frames.

Some notes regarding the newSprite API:

- The first parameter is the sprite sheet table created previously.
- The second parameter is the sequence we just created.

3) Now, change the position of the sprite and play the animation:

```
chicken1.x = display.contentCenterX
chicken1.y = display.contentCenterY * 0.3
chicken1:play()
```

If you created the sprite sheet with a tool, the process is slightly different:

1) Load the sprite sheet (see above).
2) Describe an animation and create the sprite:

```
local sequenceData2 =
{
      name="fly",
      frames={sheetInfo:getFrameIndex
             ("blitzsubspeed1"),
             sheetInfo:getFrameIndex
             ("blitzsubspeed2"),
             sheetInfo:getFrameIndex
             ("blitzsubspeed3"),
             sheetInfo:getFrameIndex
             ("blitzsubspeed4")},
      time=250,
      loopCount = 0,
      loopDirection = "bounce"
}

local chicken2 = display.newSprite(sheet_
frompacker, sequenceData2)
```

Some notes regarding the option table:

- This animation is called "fly" (*name*). In a game, some characters can use several animations: jump, run, explode, and so forth.
- The animation is described frame by frame because the texture packer tool is not intended to order the frames in their original order (we use *getFrameIndex* from the image sheet to get the index of the frame from its original name).
- Each frame is displayed 250 for milliseconds (*time*).
- The animation loops indefinitely (*loop=0*).
- The animation bounce (*loopDirection*) means that the animation will play forward then backward through the sequence of frames.

Some notes regarding the newSprite API:

- The first parameter is the sprite sheet table created previously.
- The second parameter is the sequence we just created.

3) Now, change the position of the sprite and play the animation:

```
chicken2.x = display.contentCenterX
chicken2.y = display.contentCenterY * 1.3
chicken2:play()
```

The full code sample, named "ChickenSprite," is available from the book companion.

TO GO FURTHER . . .

CoronaLabs provides a detailed guide for sprite sheets here:

http://docs.coronalabs.com/guide/media/imageSheets/index.html

There is more to learn regarding sprites and animation sequences in the newSprite API documentation:

http://docs.coronalabs.com/api/library/display/newSprite.html

Part 4
Advanced Features

Introduction

In this section, you'll learn to add "must have" features to your games:

- Organize your games in screens
- Add sounds and advanced input
- Save and restore game data

The road to creating a great, complete game is almost over!

Compose Your Screens With Composer

A real game, with the exception of something very simple or conceptual, is made up of several screens: menu, option, gameplay, and so forth. Corona SDK makes the job very easy with **Composer**, a Corona library that lets you create and manage screens, also known as "scenes."

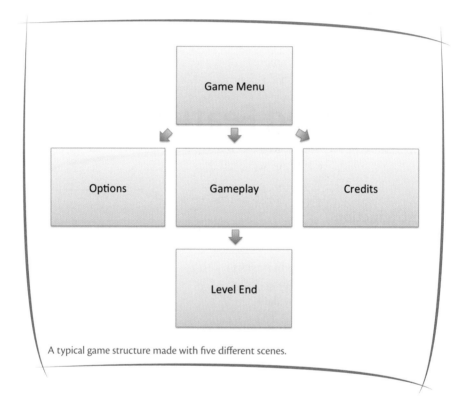

A typical game structure made with five different scenes.

Create and Open a Scene

A scene is a Lua file that provides the full structure of the scene. A scene itself is composed of events functions like "create," "destroy," and so on. Let's start with a new and empty project.

In your main.lua file, enter these two lines:

```
local composer = require("composer")
composer.gotoScene("scene1")
```

This code requires the Composer library (and assigns it to a table called *composer*) then opens the scene called "scene1."

Now, add a new Lua file to your project and call it "scene1.lua." As you can understand, the file must be named "scene1.lua" because gotoScene is opening a scene called "scene1."

Let's create a very simple scene with a single and touchable text on its center. Here is the code from "scene1.lua":

```
local composer = require("composer")

local scene = composer.newScene()

function scene:create(event)

    local sceneGroup = self.view

    local mytitle = display.newText(sceneGroup,
        "Goto scene 2!",
        display.contentCenterX,
        display.contentCenterY,
        native.systemFont,
        25)

    function onTouchText(event)
        print("Text was touched!")
    end
    mytitle:addEventListener("tap", onTouchText)
end

scene:addEventListener("create", scene)

return scene
```

Run the project and touch the text. Ok, nothing happens . . . but it's not finished! You have to understand what we did first. The "scene.lua" file is creating and returning a new scene. It's a kind of object that will then be used by *gotoScene*.

So, we first create a new scene:

```
local scene = composer.newScene()
```

Then we implement a function for the scene:

```
function scene:create(event)
...
```

> NOTE: If you're not familiar with this kind of function, take a look at the chapter "Object-Oriented Programming With Lua."

This function is called when the scene is opened, before displaying anything. So it's the perfect place to create the display object composing the screen—in our case, a text label:

```
...
    local mytitle = display.newText(self.view, ...
```

Note how the label is added to a view using the optional parent parameter from newText.

Yes, a Composer scene is a display group! The Composer library creates the group when the scene is created, so you don't have to deal with its creation. However, you do have to add all the display objects that you create to the scene view. This view is accessible in the *view* property of the scene. Just use "*self.view*" in any scene function to access it.

The following code is just adding a tap event to the label. Refer to the chapter "Moving Objects Around the Screen: The Interactive Way" if you missed something.

Finally, we link the *scene:create* function to the *create* event that will be raised by the scene:

```
scene:addEventListener("create", scene)
```

Change the Current Scene

Now that we know how to create and display a scene, let's create a second one. Add a new Lua file to your project and call it "scene2.lua."

Use the very same code for the second scene. Just change the text of the label from "Goto scene 2" to "Goto scene 1":

```
local mytitle = display.newText(sceneGroup,
        "Goto scene 1!",
        display.contentCenterX,
        display.contentCenterY,
        native.systemFont,
        25)
```

You can now guess the plan: go to scene 2 from scene 1 and . . . go to scene 1 from scene 2! Let's add the "go to" stuff to our code now.

In "scene1.lua," just change the onTouchText function to match this:

```
function onTouchText(event)
        composer.gotoScene("scene2")
end
```

And in "scene2.lua":

```
function onTouchText(event)
        composer.gotoScene("scene1")
end
```

Run your code. You can now jump from one scene to another!

It's Just the Beginning

This chapter demonstrated just a small part of Composer. We'll use some advanced features from Composer in the next chapter, but here are the things you need to know:

Additionally to *create*, the scenes are exposing 3 other events:

```
scene:show()
```

This event is raised after the create event, when the scene will be shown. It's the best place to add some effects to the display objects (such as fade-in or transitions).

```
scene:hide()
```

This event is raised when the scene is hidden because another scene is opening.

```
scene:destroy()
```

This event is raised when the scene is destroyed. Composer is doing the job of removing the displayed object attached to the scene view. So this event is useful to execute a special treatment, like undoing something you did in the create event.

The show and hide events are raised twice: once when Composer is about to do the job (show or hide), and once after Composer does the job. You can use the event parameter, passed to the function, to test which phase is triggered. This *event* included a *phase* parameter:

```
function scene:show(event)
        if (event.phase == "will") then
            -- Your code here, executed before
        the scene is shown
            elseif (event.phase == "did") then
            -- Your code here, executed after
        the scene is shown
        end
end

scene:addEventListener("show", scene)
```

Practice

Now, it's quite easy to add the show event to our scene. Do not forget the addEventListener at the end!

Then, make the title fade in when the scene is displayed.

The idea is simple:

- Make the title become invisible (alpha=0) before the scene is displayed.
- Transition the title alpha to 1 when the scene is displayed.

TO GO FURTHER . . .

You can find a scene template in the official Composer documentation:

http://docs.coronalabs.com/api/library/composer/index.html

A full guide provides in-depth details here:

http://docs.coronalabs.com/guide/system/composer/index.html

Add Sounds and Music

Take a breath. We will now discuss a very simple feature: sounds. Although playing a sound is very easy with Corona SDK, it's not always easy to find or create sounds. Here are some tips.

What Is a Sound?

In the game programmer universe, a sound is a file containing some sound data. Corona supports a few different sound file formats, but to have a fully cross-platform game, please use only MP3 and WAV.

A WAV sound is heavy; an MP3 sound is light.

You get the point: MP3 is the better sound format for your games.

On the tool side, there is one must-have: Audacity. This is an audio editor that's useful for cutting, converting, or tweaking your sounds. It is available for both Windows and Mac, and you can download it for free here:

http://audacity.sourceforge.net/

Create a Sound

The purest way to get sound effects is to create them yourself! You can record some sounds, or create your sounds using tools, but that's out of our scope here.

However, if you want to create some fun arcade sounds, use SFRX by Tomas Pettersson:

www.drpetter.se/project_sfxr.html

This tool will help you create random arcade sounds with just a few mouse clicks.

Download or Buy a Sound

If you're not comfortable with sound creation, try free sounds on the Internet, or buy professional game sounds for a low fee. Do an Internet search for "free sounds." For professional sounds, including a great selection for game developers, I recommend www.soundrangers.com. Nice guys with nice, cheap sounds.

Play a Sound, the Straight Way

There are two simple ways to play a sound: stream sounds or regular sounds. Both use the same library called "audio."

Stream sounds are loaded in little chunks and do not use a lot of memory. They're mostly used for background music.

Load and play a stream sound:

```
local myGameMusic = audio.loadStream("mymusic.
mp3")
audio.play(myGameMusic)
```

Regular sounds are loaded in their entirety. It's the best way to incorporate event sounds.

Load and play a regular sound:

```
local shootSound = audio.load("shoot.mp3")
audio.play(shootSound)
```

In the example, the load and loadStream are receiving the name of the sound file, and return a handle (or "channel number" in some documentation). You then just have to pass this handle to audio.play.

> TIP: Load your sounds beforehand; for example, during the scene creation.

Play a Sound, the Advanced Way

You can pass a table containing parameters to audio.play to decide some of the behavior, and you can use the sound handle to do some magic things, like changing the volume. Here are the different use cases you need to learn:

Loop a Sound

```
audio.play(myGameMusic, { loops= -1})
```

or

```
local options = {
     loops = -1
}
audio.play(myGameMusic, options)
```

Execute a Code When the Playback Ends

```
local function soundIsDone(event)
      print("The sound ends and its name
was",event.name)
end
local options = {
      onComplete(soundIsDone)
}
audio.play(myGameMusic, options)
```

Pause and Resume a Sound or Music

Example: playing and pausing the background music:

```
audio.play(myGameMusic, { loops= -1})
...
audio.pause(myGameMusic)
```

And later, to resume the music:

```
audio.resume(myGameMusic)
```

Change the Sound Volume

Set the master volume to 50%:

```
audio.setVolume(0.5)
```

Set the volume for a specific sound:

```
audio.setVolume(0.75, { channel=myGameMusic })
```

Practice

You are on vacation, no need to practice today!

TO GO FURTHER . . .

You can find the entire audio library API in the official documentation:
http://docs.coronalabs.com/api/library/audio/index.html

And an official guide here:
http://docs.coronalabs.com/guide/media/audioSystem/index.html

Menu and User Interface

What do you think of what you have learned so far? You have learned everything you need to create your own games by displaying things, make them move, and making noise . . . but now you need to learn how to put it all into a nice box!

The box is the User Interface (UI), also known as the Head Up Display (HUD) by the pros. The main part of this HUD is the game menu. All the remaining screens will be similar.

I'm going to show you how to create a **nice animated menu**. Here is our objective, with around 80 lines of code:

You can create this nice menu with just 80 lines of code.

> NOTE: You can use your own graphic assets, but for the example I
> used some of my own, inspired by my game Chicken Deep. You can
> download these assets from the book companion and use them for
> testing purposes.
>
> Also note that this example is for a smartphone, not for an iPad. To
> understand the specifics of iPad programming, please refer to the next
> chapter.

Support the Retina Display

The Apple Retina screen doubles the number of pixels on the screen. If
you use non-Retina assets on a Retina device, your game will be blurry.
And that's not counting the hundreds of different Android screen sizes.
Luckily, Corona SDK supports multiple screen size resolutions, including Retina!

For this menu, we will support the Retina display. We'll go deeper into
this subject in the next chapter.

To begin, look at your config.lu file and make sure it contains the
imageSuffix keyword, like this:

```
application = {
      content = {
              width = 320,
              height = 480,
              scale = "letterBox",
              fps = 60,

  imageSuffix = {
                  ["@2x"] = 2,
                  }
          },
}
```

Then, provide your images in two versions:

- An original version; for example: "background.jpg"
- A version that is twice the size, with the suffix @2x at the end of the
  file name, example "background@2x.jpg"

How Does This Work?

The Corona engine will choose the correct graphics for you according to the resolution of the platform on which the app is running.
Example:

- Your app is based on a 320x480 device (config.lua settings).
- You app runs on a Retina device, which means a 640x960 resolution.
- Corona SDK calculates the ratio between the original resolution and the real one: the ratio is x2!
- Corona will use the @2x versions of your assets if they exist.

Last requirement: use *newImageRect* and not *newImage* to ensure the support of the dynamic resolution.

The Background Picture

Create a project with two empty scenes: menu and gameplay. Then open the menu from the main.lua file, like this:

```
-- From main.lua
local composer = require("composer")
composer.gotoScene("menu", "fade")
```

Now, create the *menu.lua* scene and modify the **create** function to match this:

```
local view = self.view

-- Main background
local background = display.newImageRect(view,
"background.jpg", 320, 568)
background.x = display.contentCenterX
background.y = display.contentCenterY
```

I have chosen a 320×568 pixel background, which will support most of the Android screen sizes, and will perfectly support the 3.5-inch iPhone 4 screen, the 4-inch iPhone 5 screen, and the recent iPhone 6 and iPhone 6 plus screen ratio.

The Game Logo

We'll now display an image logo on the upper part of the screen:

```
-- Game Logo
menuLogo = display.newImageRect(view, "logo.
png", 252, 124)
menuLogo.x = display.contentCenterX
menuLogo.y = 130
```

The Play Button

I chose to display the play button over a nice, animated overlay:

```
menuOverlay = display.newImageRect(view,
"overlay.png", 320, 180)
menuOverlay.anchorY = 1
menuOverlay.x = display.contentCenterX
menuOverlay.y = display.actualContentHeight +
display.screenOriginY

menuButton = display.newImageRect(view, "play.
png", 146, 69)
menuButton.x = display.contentCenterX
menuButton.y = 390 - display.screenOriginY
```

Note how the overlay and the button are displayed relative to the bottom of screen. We use here the *display.screenOriginY* value provided by Corona SDK. In our example, this value is 0 if we run the app on an iPhone 4 and 44 on an iPhone 5. Indeed, the iPhone 5 is 88 pixels higher than the iPhone 4 (44 is half of 88).

NOTE: Relative to the Retina resolution, this difference is 176 (88×2).

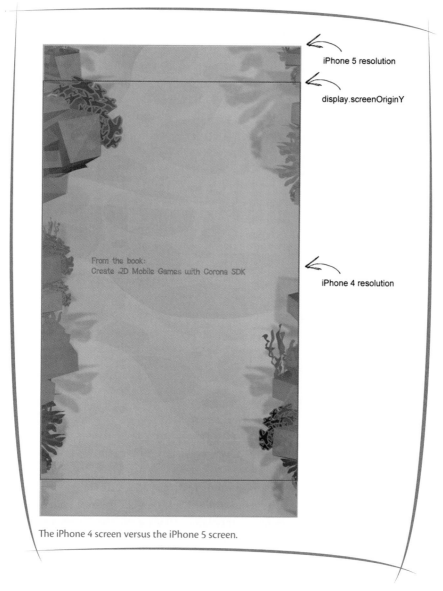

iPhone 5 resolution

display.screenOriginY

iPhone 4 resolution

From the book:
Create 2D Mobile Games with Corona SDK

The iPhone 4 screen versus the iPhone 5 screen.

Add Some Fishes

We'll make some fun fishes appear in the center of the screen:

```
menuFish = display.newImageRect(view, "fish.png",
68, 39)
menuFish.x = display.contentCenterX
menuFish.y = display.contentCenterY
```

Add Interactivity

We now have to react when the play button is pressed. You know how:

```
function onPlay(event)
      composer.gotoScene("gameplay", options)
end
menuButton:addEventListener("tap", onPlay)
```

This code will open the gameplay scene when the button is tapped. For the example, you have to create a *gameplay.lua* scene.

Animate the Menu

To make the menu appealing, we'll add some animation:

- Animate the overlay, then display the button with a nice fade-in effect.
- Make the fishes swim.

The principle is quite simple. We'll hide the overlay and the button before the scene is displayed:

```
function scene:show(event)
      if (event.phase == "will") then
            print("will")
            menuOverlay.isVisible = false
            menuButton.isVisible = false
            menuFish.x = display.
actualContentWidth + menuFish.width
   . . .
```

As you can see, before the scene is displayed (*phase == "will"*), we make the overlay and the button invisible (*.isVisible = false*), and we move the fish out of the screen.

Then, when the scene is shown, we start the animations:

```
   . . .
elseif (event.phase == "did") then
      print("did")
      menuOverlay.isVisible = true
```

```
local function showButton()
        menuButton.isVisible = true
        menuButton.alpha = 0
        transition.fadeIn(menuButton,
{time=500})
    end
    transition.from(menuOverlay,
{time=500,y=menuOverlay.y+menuOverlay.
height, transition=easing.outQuad,
onComplete=showButton})
    local function moveFish()
        if menuFish.x < 0-menuFish.width
then
            menuFish.x = display.
actualContentWidth + menuFish.width
        end
        transition.to(menuFish, {time=1500,
x=menuFish.x-50, transition=easing.inOutQuad,
onComplete=moveFish})
    end
    transition.to(menuFish, {time=1500,
x=menuFish.x-50, transition=easing.inOutQuad,
onComplete=moveFish})
end
```

Despite the large amount of code, it's not a big deal. We're using the transitions to make the animation, using the onComplete callback to chain the animation:

- The overlay is slid from the bottom of the screen, and then the button is displayed when the transition is completed.
- The fish are moved from the right to the left with a nice effect, then moved back to the right when they are out of the screen.

Practice

Download the full sample from the book companion website, then analyze the code to see how it works. Look how I made the fish swim by chaining transitions.

I passed a parameter from the menu to the gameplay scene using the *params* property:

```
local options =
{
effect = "fade",
      time = 300,
      params = {
            sampleParam = "I was here!"
      }
}
composer.gotoScene("gameplay", options)
```

Then the parameter is retrieved and displayed from the gameplay scene:

```
function scene:show(event)
      if (event.phase == "will") then
            print("will")
            myTitle.alpha = 0

            print("Get a parameter:",event.
params.sampleParam)
. . .
```

TO GO FURTHER . . .

Read carefully the documentation regarding newImageRect to get more detail about the dynamic content scaling:
http://docs.coronalabs.com/api/library/display/newImageRect.html

Some more information regarding the iPad and the Retina display:
http://coronalabs.com/blog/2012/03/22/developing-for-ipad-retina-display/

The Screen Jungles

We briefly mentioned in the previous chapter how difficult it is to support multiple screen resolutions. Yet today, apps should run in full screen to be the most appealing. Although Corona SDK helps a lot, it's still difficult to understand all the refinements of this topic.

In this chapter I'm going to give you some tips on how Corona SDK supports multiple resolutions, and we'll finish with a sample showing you how to support smartphones and tablets.

The Content Area

The minimal config.lua, and the one generated by the Corona Simulator when you create a new project, look almost identical:

```
application = {
        content = {
                width = 320,
                height = 480,
                scale = "letterBox",
                fps = 60,

                imageSuffix = {
                        ["@2x"] = 2,
                }
        },
}
```

The *width* and the *height* are defining the **content area.** This content area represents the virtual size of the app you are creating. It's virtual, because the actual device resolution will differ most of the time. Corona will then use the scale factor, defined by *scale*, to adjust the content area size and the aspect ratio to match the actual device size.

There are three possible values for the *scale* property:

- **letterBox**
  Scales the content area to fill the screen and maintain the aspect ratio. Some parts of the screen should remain empty if the app ratio differs with the device. It's like showing a 4:3 movie on a 16:9 TV.
- **zoomEven**
  Scales the content to fill the *whole* screen, even if some parts fall outside of the screen. The aspect ratio is still maintained.
- **zoomStretch**
  Scales the content to fill the whole screen, and distorts the content area to match the device screen size. It's like stretching the 4:3 movie to fill your 16:9 TV screen. I'm sure you've done this! You have to know the truth: It's bad and it's ugly.

Now that you know the three possible values, forget the last two, and use only **letterBox**.

A Full-Screen App: The Old Way

Here is how to create a full-screen app using the old way.

Why do I call this the "old" way? Because it's how we used to do it until a user named @aukStudios on the Coronalabs forum created a special config.lua simplifying the process (this was enhanced by Rob Miracle from Corona Labs in a recent Tutorial—see "To Go Further" below).

Why do I show you this if it's an "old" way? Because this will show you the internal mechanics of Corona SDK for supporting multiple screen sizes. It's good to know how an engine works. So please create a new project and let Corona Simulator create the config.lua for you, or download the "JungleScreen" sample on the companion book web site.

In the official JungleScreen sample, I created a special background to show you the bleed part of the screen (the part that can be cropped depending on the device size):

Parts can be cropped on some devices!

Activate the Retina support by uncommenting the part:

```
imageSuffix = {
      ["@2x"] = 2,
}
```

Create a high-definition 720x1140 pixel background with your favorite tool (such as Photoshop or Gimp), and call it **background@2x.jpg**. Divide its size by two (360x570 pixels) and call it **background.jpg**. Now, here is your **main.lua**:

```
-- main.lua

display.setStatusBar(display.HiddenStatusBar)

background = display.newImageRect("360x570bg.
jpg", 360, 570)
background.x = display.contentCenterX
background.y = display.contentCenterY

print("display.screenOriginX", display.
screenOriginX)
print("display.screenOriginY", display.
screenOriginY)
print("display.actualContentWidth", display.
actualContentWidth)
print("display.actualContentHeight", display.
actualContentHeight)
print("display.contentWidth", display.
contentWidth)
print("display.contentHeight", display.
contentHeight)
```

Run this code, and look at your traces. The code is displaying all the key values from the display API.

Now, imagine you want to display a red square at 10 pixels from the left side of your screen. Add these lines:

```
redSquare = display.newRect(0, 0, 50, 50)
redSquare:setFillColor(1,0,0)
redSquare.strokeWidth = 1
redSquare:setStrokeColor(0)
redSquare.anchorX = 0
redSquare.x = 10
redSquare.y = display.contentCenterY
```

Run your code and play with the "Window/View as" menu. Try the iPad, the iPhone 5, the Kindle Fire, and other platforms. Look how the values differ and how your background is cropped, or not.

Is your red square at 10 pixels from the left side on every device? No. This is because when the screen aspect ratio is different than your content area aspect ratio, some parts of the screen are cropped, and others are added with blank (actually black) content.

You can fix the issue by using the display.screenOriginX (or display.screenOriginY) property:

```
redSquare = display.newRect(0, 0, 50, 50)
redSquare:setFillColor(1,0,0)
redSquare.strokeWidth = 1
redSquare:setStrokeColor(0)
redSquare.anchorX = 0
redSquare.x = 10 + display.screenOriginX
redSquare.y = display.contentCenterY
```

Fixed! But you need to apply this to any display object you need to align with the borders. It's tedious and it's a source of bugs. The sample "ScreenJungle" shows you how to adjust the position to display objects on all four sides.

Now comes the magical config.lua . . .

The Magical Config.lua

Here it is:

```lua
local aspectRatio = display.pixelHeight /
display.pixelWidth
application = {
      content = {
            width = aspectRatio > 1.5 and 800 or
math.ceil(1200 / aspectRatio),
            height = aspectRatio < 1.5 and 1200
or math.ceil(800 * aspectRatio),
            scale = "letterBox",
            fps = 60,

            imageSuffix = {
                  ["@2x"] = 1.3,
            },
      },
}
```

What Is Magic About It?

- This config.lua supports the most recent devices, those with a high-definition screen and those without.
- This config.lua will adjust your content area to match the screen size—no more aspect ratio adjustments!
- No more need for the use of display.screenOriginX (or display.screenOriginY) because there is no blank part on the screen or cropped content area.

Are There Any Drawbacks?

Only one: You can no longer assume the width or the height of your content area, so you need to use relative positions for your assets (using display.contentWidth, display.contentHeight, etc.).

The iPhone 5 Specificity

To let Apple know that your app supports the iPhone 5, you have to provide a ***Default-568h@2x.png*** launch image file. This file is case sensitive and must be exactly 640 pixels wide and 1136 pixels high. Place it in the same folder as your main.lua. If you do not provide this, Apple will display your app as it would appear on iPhone 4!

The iPhone 6 Specificity

The recent availability of the iPhone 6 and iPhone 6 plus brings with them a new pack of specificities. Please refer to this official blog posts from Corona to support the new icons and launch images:

http://coronalabs.com/blog/2014/10/07/tutorial-working-with-the-new-iphones/

http://coronalabs.com/blog/2014/10/21/tutorial-building-multi-screen-launch-images-using-xcode-6/

TO GO FURTHER . . .

Corona SDK official documentation for the project configuration:
http://docs.coronalabs.com/guide/basics/configSettings/index.html

The tutorial from which I took the magical config.lua, including some explanation on how it happens:
http://coronalabs.com/blog/2013/09/10/modernizing-the-config-lua/

Save and Restore Data

Most games need data to be saved. Some data is relative to the game content (levels, items), while some is relative to the player (score, last position). Once again, Corona SDK makes the process quite easy.

The JSON File Format

JSON (JavaScript Object Notation) has replaced XML (Extensible Markup Language) in the world of independent game programmers. It's a way to write data in text. This text is then saved in a file. This file is then read to restore data when needed.

JSON is smart, light, easy to read and write, and is supported by almost all the programming languages.

Another strength: this format is Lua-friendly, as it perfectly mirrors the Lua tables!

Look at this Lua table:

```
gamedata = {}
gamedata.player = {}
gamedata.player.live = 3
gamedata.player.shield = 100
```

And now, translated in JSON:

```
{"player":{"live":3,"shield":100}}
```

If we add indentation, look how similar it is to the Lua table:

```
{
        "player":
        {
                "live":3,
                "shield":100
        }
}
```

Now that you're convinced, here is the developer kit to use JSON in your Corona SDK games!

Load Data for Game Content

It is sometimes clever to store some data in a text file. It's easiest to maintain, modify, and to exchange with other team members. Let's say that we're creating a space game. We need to store the ships' characteristics in a JSON file. Here's how:

The first option is to create a JSON file by hand. It's not easy because one error is fatal: your file won't be readable. But it's doable.

The smart option is to create a file template with Corona SDK, and then you'll be able to edit it, if needed, with a text editor!

Let's create a test project to generate your table:

```
local json = require "json"

ships = {}
ships[1] = {}
ships[1].name = "Alpha Centauri"
ships[1].shield = 100

ships[2] = {}
ships[2].name = "Cygnus"
ships[2].shield = 150

ships[3] = {}
ships[3].name = "Taurus"
ships[3].shield = 200

encoded = json.encode(ships)

print(encoded)
```

The encoded table (in JSON format) is then displayed in the console. Just copy and paste the text in a text editor. The result is:

```
[{"name":"Alpha Centauri","shield":100},
{"name":"Cygnus","shield":150},
{"name":"Taurus","shield":200}]
```

To read this data in your game, just use these lines of code:

```
-- Json code for external variable loading
local function jsonFile(filename,path)
      local path = system.pathForFile(filename,
path)
      local contents
      local file = io.open(path, "r")
      if file then
            contents = file:read("*a")
            io.close(file)
      end
      return contents
end

shipsData = {}
jsonContent = jsonFile("ships.json",system.
ResourceDirectory)
shipsData = json.decode(jsonContent)
```

We first declare a small function *jsonFile* able to read a text file and
return its content in a string. Then we use this function to read our
JSON file in the resource directory. The resource directory is the folder
where the game files are stored (just put files beside your Lua files so
they will be installed in the resource directory).

Once we have the file content in a string (*jsonContent* in the example),
we just have to decode it to get a Lua table containing the data!

Let's display the data we just read:

```
print("I got",#shipsData, "ships from the JSON
file")

for i in pairs(shipsData) do
            print(shipsData[i].name,shipsData[i]
.shield)
end
```

> NOTE: We just used here what we learned in the chapter "Arrays and
> Lists" to browse the array.

Save and Restore Player Data

Nice! You now know how to read some data from an existing JSON file and convert it to a Lua table. We'll now look at how to write some data to a file.

```
function saveToFile(filename, path, contents)
      local filepath = system.pathForFile
(filename, path)
      local file = io.open(filepath, "w")
      file:write(contents)
      io.close(file)
      file = nil
end

saveToFile("gamedata.json", system.DocumentsDi-
rectory, encoded)
```

It's quite similar to how we read data. The *saveToFile* function is a helper function able to write a string to a file. We then just have to write the encoded data in a file—in our case, in the DocumentsDirectory. The DocumentsDirectory is the folder where you can create files that will persist between application sessions. On iOS, this information is backed up by syncing!

TO GO FURTHER . . .

All you need to know about the Resource Directory:
http://docs.coronalabs.com/api/library/system/ResourceDirectory.html

And for the Documents Directory:
http://docs.coronalabs.com/api/library/system/DocumentsDirectory.html

And all about the JSON API from Corona SDK:
http://docs.coronalabs.com/api/library/json/index.html

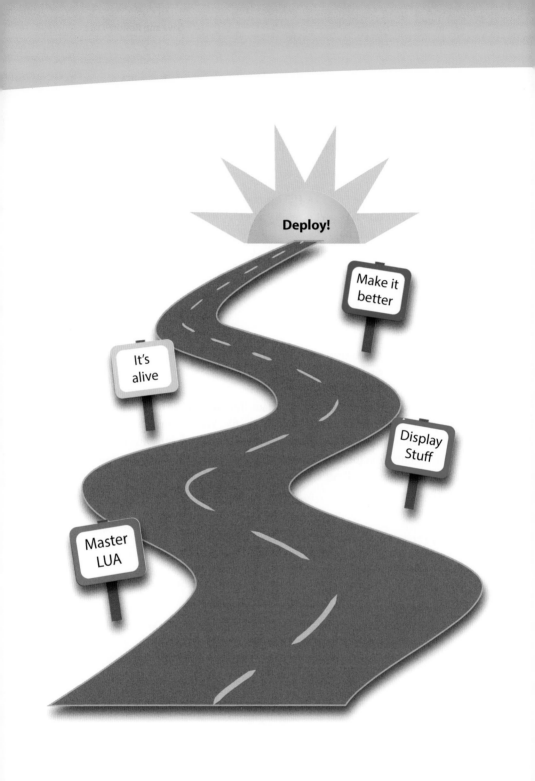

Deploy!

Make it better

It's alive

Display Stuff

Master LUA

Part 5
To the Stores

From Your Computer to the Stores

It's time to reach your players. You'll now decide how to make money, test, and debug your game, then deploy it!

Make Money With Your Games

If you want to create games just for fun, you can skip this chapter and save time and stress. If you want to earn money from your games, be prepared to work seriously on the topic.

Making money is not the fun part, and if you plan to integrate In-App Purchases into your games, it can be quite tricky. Thanks to Corona SDK, however, the technical part is made much easier.

My idea in this chapter is to paint a picture of the different ways to make money, and show you some code snippets to integrate In-App Purchases into your games.

How to Make Money?

There are three ways to make money with your games:

- Charge for it. This kind of game is called a "premium game."
- Include paid content through In-App Purchases (IAP). This kind of game is called a "freemium game."
- Include advertisement banners in your game.

There is no perfect choice. While the freemium model seems like the new El Dorado, another model could be a better choice depending on your strategy.

Charging for Your Game

This is the simplest choice, technically speaking. You make this choice when you add your game to the store. This makes your game design and coding a lot easier because you won't have to calibrate your gameplay to convince your players to pay. However, you have to convince your players in advance. It's the traditional way to sell games, and many games are still making money in this way, against the current trend of the freemium model.

Include Paid Content: In-App Purchases

Have you ever made a payment from within a game from your iPhone or your Android device? You should note the different kind of purchases:

- You pay for virtual money/currency.
- You pay to unlock a feature or the full game content.

> **NOTE:** I do not cover subscription purchases here; these are too far from the game universe.

These kinds of purchases have different names depending on the vendor:

	APPLE	GOOGLE PLAY
Virtual currency	Consumable	Unmanaged Product
Feature / full game	Non-Consumable	Managed Product

Before proposing IAP in your game, you need to set up the products in the developer's portals. Each product has an identifier (ID) that you then use in your code. The standard is to use the "reverse domain name" system:

com.yourcompany.yourgame.yourproduct

To set up your respective developer's account, follow the updated processes from the CoronaLabs documentation:

iOS:

http://docs.coronalabs.com/daily/guide/monetization/IAP/index.html#setupios

Google Play:

http://docs.coronalabs.com/daily/guide/monetization/IAP/index.html#google-play-setup

You will then use the store API from Corona SDK through three main API calls:

- store.init()
- store.purchase()
- store.restore()

I definitely encourage you to learn from the Corona Labs documentation and to experiment. I cannot show you everything here, but I've given you the fundamentals.

Here are some useful code snippets for reference:

Initialize the Store

For iOS:

```
local store = require("store")
store.init("apple", storeTransaction)
```

For Google Play:

```
local store = require("store")
store.init("google", storeTransaction)
```

The storeTransaction callback is an all-in-one function taking care of transaction process and result:

```
function transactionCallback(event)

    local transaction = event.transaction

    if transaction.state == "purchased" then

        -- Transaction successful

    elseif transaction.state == "restored" then

        -- Transaction restored

    elseif transaction.state == "cancelled" then

        -- Transaction cancelled

    elseif transaction.state == "failed" then

        -- Transaction failed

    else

    end

    store.finishTransaction(transaction)
end
```

Depending on the event.transaction value, you'll get some useful properties.

SUCCESSFUL OR RESTORED TRANSACTION	
transaction.productIdentifier	The product identifier associated with the transaction.
transaction.receipt	A JSON string receipt that can be used to verify the purchase. This is the "inapp_signed_data" returned by Google Play.
transaction.signature	A digital signature string that can be used to verify the purchase. This is the "inapp_signature" returned by Google Play. Returns nil on iOS.
transaction.identifier	A unique transaction identifier returned from the store. It is a string.
transaction.date	The date when the transaction occurred.
RESTORED TRANSACTION	
transaction.originalReceipt	Same as the receipt, but for the original purchase.
transaction.originalIdentifier	Same as the identifier, but for the original purchase.
transaction.originalDate	Same as the date, but for the original purchase.
FAILED TRANSACTION	
transaction.errorType	The type of error that occurred when the state is "failed" (a string).
transaction.errorString	A more descriptive error message of what went wrong in the "failed" case.

All these values are related to the vendor, and you should read the official documentation from them to get more details:

For iOS:

https://developer.apple.com/library/mac/documentation/NetworkingInternet/Conceptual/StoreKitGuide/Introduction.html

For Google Play:

http://developer.android.com/guide/market/billing/billing_admin.html

Make a Purchase

```
store.purchase(productList)
```

The product list can contain a single product or several products. Example for a single product:

```
store.purchase({"com.yourcompany.yourgame.
yourproduct"})
```

Restore a Purchase

```
store.restore()
```

Restoring a purchase is sometimes needed when the player installs your game on a new device. It's not relative to consumable products.

> IMPORTANT: From the Android side, do not forget to add the permissions in the build.settings file:

```
android =

{
  usesPermissions =
  {
    "android.permission.INTERNET",
    "com.android.vending.BILLING",
    "com.android.vending.CHECK_LICENSE",
  },
},
```

Include Advertisement Banners

Corona SDK has partnerships with many ad providers, so you have many choices: AdMob, iAds, InMobi, inneractive, Vungle, CrossInstall, and others. You can find the supported networks in the ads API documentation:

http://docs.coronalabs.com/daily/api/library/ads/index.html

Most of the time, displaying ads is very easy, using a couple of functions. First you have to initialize the ad network:

```
ads.init()
```

> NOTE: How you will set up then initialize the ad network will depend on the partner. I won't cover all the partners here; please refer to the Corona SDK documentation.

Then, display and hide the banners:

```
ads.show()
ads.hide()
```

There are also other ad network partners that are not part of the ads API. For instance, the Chartboost community provides an open source plugin on their official site: https://help.chartboost.com/documentation/open-source-sdks#corona. So, be aware and keep up with the Corona Labs forums.

Expect to spend a lot of effort finding players, as making money with ads requires A LOT of active players!

Then, you just have to collect the money!

TO GO FURTHER . . .

Corona Labs provides a complete guide for In-App Purchases:
http://docs.coronalabs.com/daily/guide/monetization/IAP/index.html

And a tutorial:
http://coronalabs.com/blog/2013/09/03/tutorial-understanding-in-app-purchases/

Do not forget the store API documentation to get detailed samples for each function:
http://docs.coronalabs.com/api/library/store/index.html

As the rules are changing often, you should always refer to the official Corona SDK documentation regarding topics linked to the Apple and Google stores.

Regarding In-App Advertising, here is the complete list of the supported networks and how to implement them:
http://docs.coronalabs.com/api/library/ads/index.html

Test and Debug

At the beginning of this book, I explained how to trace some comments in the simulator console. I'll now elaborate on that and give you some tips to test and debug your app like a pro.

There are two kinds of bugs:

- Syntax bugs: There is a typo in your code. Most of the time, the Corona Simulator will display the error in the console or a dialog box.
- Programming bugs: The simulator does not display a message, but the program is doing weird things: some values are wrong, the game does not respond, and so forth.

Syntax bugs are easy to fix. The message from the simulator is quite clear, providing the line number along with some information:

```
Corona Simulator Runtime error
/BouncingBall/main.lua:10: attempt to call field
'starte' (a nil value)
stack traceback:
/BouncingBall/main.lua:10: in main chunk
```

The code was:

```
physics.starte()
```

instead of:

```
physics.start()
```

Programming bugs can be tricky to fix, and so I'll spend more time talking about them here.

Why Test and Debug?

For a game programmer, bugs are the devil. Yet, fixing bugs is the main part of the job. If I take a close look at how my time is spent when I program, a large part is dedicated to hunting down bugs. This is why I built some strategies to isolate bugs in my code.

You'll introduce bugs in your code—it's life. So expect to spend some time testing and debugging. You *test* to trigger the hidden bugs. You *debug* to isolate these bugs and fix them.

Pro Tips to Avoid Bugs

Follow these rules and you'll introduce fewer bugs into your code.

Write Readable Code

Let's imagine you have to sell your code to someone else. Is your code readable? If not, will it be readable to you some weeks later?

There are some simple rules for having readable code:

- Use explicit names for your variables and functions.
- Do not use plurals, otherwise, you'll forever ask yourself, "is there an 's' or not?"

Use a Coding Convention of Your Own, or Follow This One

- The first word of variables and functions is lowercase, and all following words start with capital letters: *myFunction*, *thisIsAVariableName*.
- Apply Hungarian Notation, which consists of starting the name with a letter describing its type: bStarted (Boolean), nLife (numeric), sName (string), fAngle (float), tPlayer (table), and so on.
- Do not introduce useless empty lines.
- Use comments to organize your code (different parts, phases, behavior, objectives, etc.), and comment to explain something, not simply repeat what your code is doing.
- Be homogenous.
- Delete commented/deactivated code.

Execute Your Code in Your Head

It's sometimes very efficient to just read your code and follow its behavior mentally.

Do Not Trust Your Code

You type some code, you run it, and it works! Some days later, someone reports a bug in this very section that you trusted so much.

I've seen too many coders say, "I trust this part, I tested it," and start digging somewhere else . . . only to find that the bug was in the part they trusted!

Even if your code seems perfect, you have to treat it with suspicion. If your code is as perfect as you think, there should be no bugs. Yet, there are some. Admit it.

It's not a treasure; it's just some lines of code! Put some traces in it, and admire the disaster . . . Most of the time, the bugs are in the places you don't expect. Be your own worst enemy: *do not trust your code*!

Use Traces

Following the previous advice, the use of traces will show you the real behavior of your code, not the one you imagined.

Sometimes, the good result you get with your code is a coincidence: the code is not always executed as you think, yet you get the result you expected, because of an unexpected side effect from another line of code!

Learn From Your Mistakes

Nothing to add . . . Just learn from your mistakes, and learn to know yourself.

Do the Monkey

Run your app and test it. Everything OK? Now, think of yourself like a monkey in the zoo. Test it again, but instead of testing like a well-behaved child, just tap everywhere like mad and . . . it's a miracle; you found a bug!

Use an Internal Version Number

```
internal_version = "1.01"
```

Display this version number somewhere in your app (in the credit scene, for instance). It's VERY useful: when a bug is reported, you will easily know the version of your app in which the bug appeared!

Make Real People Test Your Game

You can use a service like TestFlight (http://testflightapp.com/) to distribute your game to some friends or beta testers. Other people have no pity.

As humans and game programmers, most of the time we don't really test our games in depth, because we simply do not want to find bugs! Other people will do a better job.

Pro Advice to Isolate Bugs

You've got a bug, but you don't know how it happens in your code, and where it appears. How frustrating! But don't start searching everywhere and nowhere at the same time.

There is a magical way to isolate a bug: by the process of elimination.

1) Deactivate all the useless code around the part you suspect (even if your app is then partially unusable).
2) Run your code and notice that the bug is not triggered.
3) Activate a small part of the deactivated code, and run it again.
4) Proceed until the bug returns; you now know where it is hiding!

If this method does not work, consider adding dirty and temporary traces in your code: trace the suspected (and the less suspected) values, trace all the function calls, and so forth. Be patient.

Traces Are Nice

You now know how I love traces. They offer one of the simplest ways to debug.

Here are some code snippets for traces:

```
-- Trace a numeric value
print("The value x is", x)

-- Trace a string
print("My string contains", str)

-- Trace several values
print("The player lost", nDamage, "from the
level", sLevelName)
-- or
print("The player lost "..tostring(nDamage).."
from the level "..sLevelName)
```

Note how it's simplest to use commas to separate values instead of concatenating using the double dot.

One of the main issues with traces is that they will be displayed even when the game is run on a device. This consumes some of the device's performance and isn't quite clean.

My preferred method is to use a clone of the print function, which I call _print, and declare it in the main.lua file as follows:

```
-- Empty print function on device
_print = nil
-- Debug mode (set to false to deactivate traces)
DEBUG = true
if DEBUG == true then
       print("DEBUG MODE FOR PRINT ACTIVATED")
       _print = function (...)
              -- Call the regular print function
              print(…)
       end
else
       _print = function (...)
              -- nothing!
       end
end
```

Now, you have to use _print(. . . instead of print(…, and your traces won't be computed if you set the DEBUG variable to *false*. Example:

```
_print("This is a debug trace")
```

TO GO FURTHER . . .

Corona Labs has a simple tutorial about basic testing and debugging:

http://coronalabs.com/blog/2013/07/09/tutorial-basic-debugging/

Debug

Now that you've tested your game, I will teach you everything about debugging.

Debug Step by Step

If the previous debugging methods failed, it's sometimes useful to use the Corona SDK debugger. It allows you to set breakpoints and inspect variables live, while the code is running in the Corona Simulator.

> NOTE: This debugger is for more experienced developers, so you should expect to spend some time mastering this tool.

1) From the Corona Editor (understand: from Sublime Text), add a breakpoint on the line you want the code to pause at. Place your cursor on this line and open the menu Corona Editor/Corona Debugger/Toggle Breakpoint. (Repeat the process to remove a breakpoint). You can use "Right click / Toggle Breakpoint" as well, on the line you want the breakpoint.
2) Open the menu Corona Editor/Corona Debugger/Run. The editor switches in debugger mode and displays the local variables and the code stack.
3) The code is started and the debugger pauses on the first line of the project. Open the menu Corona Editor/Corona Debugger/Run again to reach the breakpoint.
4) You can now inspect variables: double-click on the variable name, then Right click/Inspect variable. Nice!
5) Step forward in your code with F11 (step over) or Shift+F11 (step into).

Test and Debug in the XCode Simulator (iOS)

If XCode is installed (and updated!) on your Mac, you'll be able to run your app in a real iOS simulator. It's a good way to check if your game is running fine before deploying it to a real device.

By "real," I mean that the Corona Simulator is a Corona Labs tool; it simulates a device but does not embed the real operating system from that device. The XCode Simulator is running the real operating system, and is very close to the real device.

To run in the XCode Simulator, follow these steps:

- Run your code in the Corona Simulator.
- From the simulator, open the menu: File/Build/iOS (or Command+b).
- Select "Build For: XCode Simulator," then "Build."
- After the build process, the XCode Simulator will run, and the Corona Simulator displays:

Get prepared for a real test on the XCode Simulator.

- Ignore this message and switch to the XCode Simulator!

For more information on the use of the XCode Simulator, refer to:
https://developer.apple.com/library/ios/documentation/IDEs/
Conceptual/iOS_Simulator_Guide/Introduction/Introduction.html

To view the traces and errors while your game is running in the XCode Simulator, just run the "Console" application. This application is installed on your Mac by default; use Spotlight to find it.

Please note that you need a provisioning profile to build an app; see the next chapter, "Deploy."

Test and Debug on Device

The last part of your job is to run your games on some real devices! How to deploy your games is described in the next chapter, "Deploy," but here I will give you some tips on how to trace and debug with a real device.

Debug on an iOS Device

- Deploy your game on your test device with an ad hoc provisioning profile.
- Run XCode, and from the "Window" menu in Xcode, choose "Organizer."
- Connect your device to your computer and select it in the Devices section (left column).
- Click the button that says "Use device for development." Once that's done, click on the "Console" link in the left column, below your device, and view your console messages there.

Debug on an Android Device

Deploying your game on Android is trickier and command-line oriented, yet it is still very simple:

- Deploy your game on your test device with the Android debug keystore.
- Install some free tools from Google (the Android Debug Bridge tools). For details on this, please see the Android Signing and Building guide from Corona Labs. (Scroll to the "Debugging" section at the bottom.)
- Connect your Android device to your computer.
- Use the ADB command-line tools from a terminal to view all the traces from your device:

```
adb logcat
```

Note that you may have to put your device into "developer mode." Do an Internet search for "android activate developer mode" to find instructions, which will depend on your device and version of Android.

TO GO FURTHER . . .

Apple explains everything about testing on a device here:

https://developer.apple.com/library/ios/documentation/IDEs/Conceptual/AppDistributionGuide/Introduction/Introduction.html

Corona Labs has published a simple tutorial about basic testing:

http://coronalabs.com/blog/2013/07/09/tutorial-basic-debugging/

The complete building guides from Corona Labs are here:

http://docs.coronalabs.com/guide/index.html#building-and-distribution

Deploy

The Holy Grail—and the most annoying and confusing part! Thanks to Corona SDK, however, deploying a game is greatly simplified.

The main thing to know is that, independently of the build/signing process, which I will explain, most of the deployment process will be different depending on the operating system (iOS or Android), the devices targeted (iPhone, iPad, Android, Kindle Fire, OUYA, etc.) and the store you want your game to be sold in. This deployment process can often evolve. That's why I will give you the fundamentals to make you autonomous and responsive, and then I'll provide you all the links to the official and updated processes.

Developer Accounts

For both iOS and Android you need a developer account.

For iOS you need an Apple ID, then register here:
https://developer.apple.com/devcenter/ios/
The current price is $99 per year.

For Android, you must sign up for a Google account, then create your Google Play developer account here:
https://play.google.com/apps/publish/signup/
The current price is $25. This is a one time registration fee.

iOS Deployment Specifics

Sorry for the bad news, but deploying for iOS is the least digestible piece of the cake. Let me elaborate:

The Provisioning Process is Tricky

You need a Developer Certificate, an App ID, registered devices to test your app, and provisioning profiles. On top of that, there are different flavors of profiles: Development, Ad Hoc, App Store . . . Did I say indigestible? Yes, it is.

Installing Apps on External Devices is Limited

If you pictured being able to build an app and send it to your friend as an email attachment, think again. You need to declare to Apple each device you need to test your app on, then create the provisioning profile again, and then build your app again.

Apple Review Is Required, and It's Serious

Apple will decide if your game deserves to be published on the store depending on some criteria. This process takes 4 or 5 days at minimum, and sometimes Apple will reject your app if it crashes or does not comply with the requirements. Hopefully, coding with Corona SDK will help you secure this validation more easily.

Android Deployment Specifics

Despite the debug process (see the previous chapter), Android is paradise for game programmers.

The Provisioning Process Is Quite Simple— After You've Done It Once!

There are no provisioning profiles here; rather, Android uses something called keystores. Corona Labs provides a debug keystore so you can build and distribute your app for testing instantly.

Installing Apps on External Devices Is Simple

There's no need to declare the devices. You can install your app on any Android device; you just need to check the option on the devices to allow external sources.

Android Validation Is Automated

Consider waiting a few hours to see your game on the store.

Build for iOS

Before building for iOS, you need to be prepared with the needed provisioning profiles.

The perfect path is:

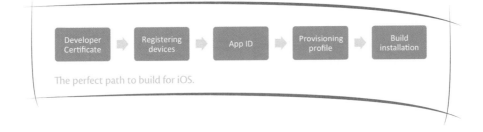

The perfect path to build for iOS.

The whole process is detailed and updated by Corona Labs in this guide:

http://docs.coronalabs.com/guide/distribution/iOSBuild/index.html

What you need to know specifically is what kind of certificates and provisioning profile you need, depending on the phase of your project. Here are the main scenarios:

Phase 1: You Want to Test the App on Your Own Devices

During the first part of your development process, you will test and debug on your own device. You'll need:

- A Development Certificate
- An iOS App Development provisioning profile

Phase 2: You Want to Distribute the App to Some (Kind) People for Testing

During this phase, you'll need to distribute test versions to real people. You'll need:

- A Development Certificate
- An Ad Hoc provisioning profile

Phase 3: You Want to Distribute the App to the App Store!

During this phase, you'll need to submit your game to the App Store. You'll require:

- A Production Certificate
- An App Store provisioning profile

> **NOTE:** Take a breath, and begin the process by following the link above, and you'll slowly become more familiar with the App Store.

Build the App

1) Run your app in the Corona Simulator.
2) Select File / Build / iOS.
3) Fill in the information:
   Application name: This defines how the app will be named on the device.

Version: A version name for your app. I suggest incrementing this version number each time you distribute your game, even for testers. Use clear names, like "beta1" for beta versions.

Build for: Select Xcode Simulator to run your app on the real Apple simulator or Device to deploy on a device.

Supported devices: You have the choice between iPhone + iPad (Universal), iPhone only, or iPad only depending on your needs.

Code signing identity: Select the appropriate provisioning profile (see below).

Save to folder: This is where to save the .app file, which is what you'll distribute!

4) Click Build!

Corona Labs servers will compile and deliver the app to you in a short time. You'll then obtain a file with the extension .app. Keep it safe!

Install on Your Own Devices

You can use either XCode Organizer or iTunes.

From XCode, choose Window / Organizer. Choose your device (you need to be connected!), and then select the Applications option. Just drag the app in the frame content and you're done.

From iTunes, choose File / Add to Library. Then select the app file. You just have to sync the device to install the app.

Install on Beta Tester Devices

Use a free online service like Testflightapp (http://testflightapp.com); it will do most of the job for you.

Build for Android

1) Run your app in the Corona Simulator.
2) Select File / Build / Android.
3) Fill in the information:

Application name: This defines how the app will be named on the device.

Version code: A numeric version number for your app. I suggest incrementing this version number each time you distribute your game, even for testers.

Version name: A version name for your app. Use clear names, like "beta1" for beta versions.

Package: The package name. The traditional Java scheme is to use the reverse-domain format like *com.yourcompany.yourapp.* Choose it carefully.

Minimum SDK version: Select the latest version.

Target app store: Select the store you're targeting. Google Play is the official store for Android phones and devices.

Keystore: Choose Debug to build for testing. Otherwise, you should create a Keystore to deploy for the stores. See "To Go Further . . ." below.

Key alias: Choose "androiddebugkey" to build for testing. Otherwise choose the alias of your app, the one you created in the Keystore.

Save to folder: This is where to save the .app file, which is what you'll distribute!

4) Click Build!

Corona Labs servers will compile and deliver the app to you in a short time. You'll then obtain a file with the extension .apk. Keep it safe!

Install on Your Own Devices or Beta Testers' Devices

Just copy the APK on the device and open it to install it. On Mac, you should install the official tool from Google:

www.android.com/filetransfer/

Then, to open the APK from the device, you have to install a file browser app like ES File Explorer File Manager.

The other way is to upload the APK to the web and provide the link to the tester. Just open the link from a device and the miracle occurs.

Deploy to the Stores

Deploying to the stores is out of the scope of this book (not to mention that the process is always evolving). However, here are some tips:

For the App Store

- To deploy on the App Store, you have to sign your app, prepare the store listing, and then submit the app.

- To prepare the store listing, go to http://itunesconnect.apple.com.
- To submit the app, use the tool "Application Loader" from your Mac.

For Google Play

- To deploy to the Google Play store, you have to build your app using a real Keystore, prepare the store listing and then submit the app.
- For the Keystore, refer to "To Go Further . . ." below for guidance.
- To prepare the store listing and submit the app, go to https://play.google.com/apps/publish/.

> PRO TIP: Target Android first. It's the shorter way and it allows reaching real players in a timely manner. The iOS publishing process is boring and long, so when you start it you'll be prepared with an improved app, thanks to the Android players.

TO GO FURTHER . . .

There are a lot of reference materials, forums, and guides on the Internet. However, the Corona Labs website remains the best place to go.

Regarding the project settings:

http://docs.coronalabs.com/guide/distribution/buildSettings/index.html

Regarding building for iOS and Android:

http://coronalabs.com/resources/tutorials/building-and-distribution/

For the Android Keystore, the process is here:

http://docs.coronalabs.com/guide/distribution/androidBuild/index.html#signrelease

The official signing documentation for Android:

http://developer.android.com/tools/publishing/app-signing.html

Finally, there are the official guides from Apple regarding the App Store:

https://developer.apple.com/appstore/index.html

More With Corona SDK?

So, you think it's over? Not at all! Corona SDK is an amazing and powerful tool that's growing every month. In this next-to-last chapter, I'd like to provide an overview of what you can still do to improve your creations, and some links to get even more out of these features.

Widgets: Create Amazing User Interfaces

Corona SDK game interfaces can be more than text and buttons.

The widget API provides a lot of widgets to create amazing and very professional user interfaces, such as:

- Picker wheel
- Progress view
- Scroll view
- Segmented controls
- Slider
- Spinner
- Stepper
- Tab bar
- Table view (the most powerful widget!)

All of these widgets are well documented in this official guide:

http://docs.coronalabs.com/api/library/widget/index.html

Mail, Facebook, and Twitter: Add Social Features

Tweeting a string is so easy with Corona SDK. Here is the simplest way:

```
local options = {
      -- 140 characters only
      message = "I'm reading an amazing book and
now I'm a game coder!"
}
native.showPopup("twitter", options)
```

This is almost the same code to send an email:

```
local options =
{
      to = "",
      subject = "This is the subject",
```

```
        body = "I'm reading an amazing book\n\
nNow I'm a game coder!"
    }
native.showPopup("mail", options)
```

Note how I included some extra lines using escape codes (\n). These two characters will then be replaced in the message by an extra line.

And now, let's publish a message on the Facebook wall of the player:

```
local fbCommand
local facebook = require("facebook")

function fbListener(event)
    print("event.name", event.name)
    print("event.type:", event.type)
    print("isError: " .. tostring(event.isError))
    print("didComplete: " .. tostring(event.
    didComplete))

    if ("session" == event.type)then
        if fbCommand == POST_MSG then
            local options = {
                name = "Message name",
                description = "I'm reading an
amazing book and now I'm a game coder!",
                listener = fbListener,
                link = "http://www.focalpress.com/"
            }

            facebook.showDialog("feed", options)
            fbCommand = nil
        end
    elseif ("request" == event.type)then
        -- event.response is a JSON object from
the FB server
        local response = event.response
```

```
    if (not event.isError) then
        response = json.decode(event.response)

        print(response)

        local alert = native.showAlert
("Facebook", "Thanks for sharing!", { "OK" })
else
    -- Post Failed, the error is stored in
event.response
    local alert = native.showAlert("Error",
"Sorry, it failed to be shared on Facebook.", {
"OK" })
        end
    end
end

fbCommand = POST_MSG
facebook.login(appId, fbListener,
{"publish_actions"})
```

> **IMPORTANT:** Facebook API needs some setup before you can use it, so please consult the official documentation to make sure you don't miss anything:
>
> http://docs.coronalabs.com/api/library/facebook/index.html
>
> For getting friends, you can also look at this official tutorial:
>
> http://coronalabs.com/blog/2014/01/14/tutorial-getting-facebook-friends-the-easy-way/

Analytics: Know Your Players

Corona SDK provides some ways to "record" any event you want that occurs in your games. This allows you to track the behavior of your player and use that data to improve your game.

This feature requires having at least a Pro version of Corona SDK and a third-party analytics provider account. At the time of writing this book, Corona SDK supports two analytics providers: Flurry and Amplitude.

Implementing analytics is very easy. Take a look at the documentation, depending on the provider you've chosen:

http://docs.coronalabs.com/api/library/analytics/

Graphics 2.0: Provide an Amazing Visual Experience

The Corona SDK graphic engine is named Graphics 2.0. It is based on OpenGL-ES 2.0 and provides some extra features if you're a paid subscriber. With it you can, for instance, distort an image to create an amazing fake 3D effect:

http://docs.coronalabs.com/guide/graphics/3D.html

Or you can add filters to your image to blur them:

http://docs.coronalabs.com/guide/graphics/effects.html

Take a look at the official advanced graphics features for more ideas:

http://docs.coronalabs.com/guide/index.html#advanced

Third-Party Plugins: Features From Partners

Corona Labs has partnered with some amazing third parties to provide powerful features for monetization, cloud-based services, multiplayer support, and so on. Some of these plugins are available to Starter subscribers, and others to Basic and Pro subscribers.

Find the complete list of plugins on this page:

http://coronalabs.com/resources/plugins/

Look at the bottom of the plugin page to find the link, "at a glance," which will display a detailed catalog of the plugins and indicate which Corona license it is running on.

Corona Enterprise or Corona Cards: The Sky's the Limit

Corona Enterprise allows you to add additional native code to your Corona SDK application. With Corona Enterprise, you definitely have no limits. Unfortunately it is reserved for advanced coders, as you'll need to know both Objective C and Java to code for iOS and Android.

In another genre, Corona Cards allows you to create native apps and games and then add Corona SDK user interfaces and features.

Everything you need to know about these different flavors of Corona SDK is on this page:

http://coronalabs.com/pricing/

Go Beyond!

You were here

Part 6
Epilog

You're done!

You've reached the end of the road, and a brand new landscape has been revealed.

However, before leaving you alone I'd like to provide you with 13 tips to help you learn and create quickly:

1—Familiarize Yourself

Read books and tutorials, open sample projects, play with the code, and try to understand it. You won't understand every line, but I have found it takes two days to begin to learn a new programming language. At this point, start coding!

2—Learn When It's Necessary

You want to work fast. So, you'll have to start programming with just some basic understanding of the language. My method: I start coding, and learn as I go along. For example, when I was developing Chicken Deep, I needed to use the accelerometer. I coded everything up until that point, and then looked at the Corona SDK documentation, and eureka, I learned all about the accelerometer!

3—Make Decisions

What is your game about? Try to sketch it on paper and divide it into chunks. I like to use wireframe templates. Start simple, create a menu scene and a gameplay scene, and use the storyboard functions of Corona.

4—Think Simple

You'll add a new scene when you need it. Don't try to plan everything, because you don't really know how your game will look before the first prototype—and even then you won't be sure!

5—Limit Yourself

Decide how many weeks you'll work on the game. The schedule will decide the features, not the other way around! Check your progress every week and make smart decisions.

6—Create From Scratch

You don't need art, sound, and music right now. Don't be shy about creating something from scratch. Use sounds from other samples or from the web. The same holds true for the art, so just use placeholders. My method is to search images with Google, adding ".png" to the search terms.

7—Prototype

Aim to prototype the gameplay in a minimum amount of time; just a few hours should be enough. If the prototype isn't great, try to enhance it. If you can't, go to sleep and try again the next day.

8—Build by Successive Refinement

A game is like a painting—you need to have something complete at every stage of its creation. Create everything, even if it's brief, and then refine each part until it's good enough to publish.

9—Integrate

When you have something playable (and demonstrable to your spouse . . .), it's time to integrate real art, music, and sounds. But don't be naïve—your game will change, up until the final version you submit to the App Store. Your inner artist needs to be aware of that.

10—Play!

Play your game at every stage. A lot.

11—Plan

Divide your process into 4 steps:

- Alpha (playable, with lot of bugs and missing features)
- Beta (few bugs, feature complete)
- Final Beta (only your spouse can ask for some changes . . .)
- Release Candidate (this is the one!)

12—Kill Your Babies

Less is more. Remove features if you feel they will impact your schedule too much, or if they make the game too complicated. I know it's hard to remove lovely lines of code, but sometimes it's for the best!

13—Take a Break

You have to stop coding at some point and decide on the release candidate.

That's it!

Thanks for reading this book. I hope you found some help and support for your game project. Do not forget to visit my book companion web site: www.create2Dmobilegames.com.

Index

advanced features 113–48; add sounds
    and music 121–4; menu and user
    interface 125–33; save and restore
    data 143–7; screen jungles 135–42
advertisement banners 154–5
anchor points 48, 51
Apple Retina 127
Apple simulator 173
arrays 30–1; browse an array 30–1;
    create an array 30; see also lists

Boolean values 12, 14
Box2D engine 89
"break" statement 26
bugs: pro advice to isolate bugs 161;
    programming 158; pro tips to avoid
    bugs 159–61; syntax 158; see also
    debug; test and debug

Chicken Deep 127, 184
collision detection 92–4, 103
combining shapes with text 60–4;
    squared title 63–4; title with a
    background 60–2; underlined
    title 63
comments 4–5, 10, 158, 159
Composer 114–19; change the current
    scene 117–18; create and open a
    scene 115–16
config.lua file 55, 82, 128, 136, 137,
    140, 141
content area 55, 136, 137, 140, 141
control structure statements: break
    statements 26; conditional state-
    ments 24–5; loop statements 25–6;
    variable scope 26–7
coordinate 44
Corona Cards 181
Corona Debugger 164
Corona Editor 10, 11, 164
Corona Enterprise 96, 181
Corona Simulator 9, 79, 136, 137, 158,
    164–5, 172, 173; TestFunctions 20

debug 163–7; Android device 166; iOS
    device 166; step by step 164; see also
    test and debug
deploy 169–75; Android deployment
    specifics 171; build for Android
    173–4; build for iOS 171–3; devel-
    oper accounts 170; iOS deployment
    specifics 170; to the stores 174–5
developer accounts 170
display 43–64; fonts 48; images 53–6;
    introduction 43–5; multiline text
    49–51; position 48; properties 45;
    shapes 57–64; texts 48–51
Documents Directory 147

easing method 71
economics 149–54; charging for your
    game 150; include advertisement
    banners 154–5; include paid content
    150–4; make money with your
    games 150
energy 15, 18, 20
EnterFrame event 84–4, 85
event listener 76–85; tap event 76;
    touch event 76–7; touch event to
    drag an object on the screen 78–9
expressions 13–15

Facebook 179–80
"fly" 107, 109
fonts 48, 50, 62, 63; custom 51
"for" 25, 28, 30
frame 82–5; EnterFrame event 82–3;
    moving a ball every frame 83–4;
    warning 85–6
functions: example 18; getting parame-
    ters and returning a value 19–20; in
    a table 20; as a task 18–19

Google 19, 170, 184; free tools 166;
    Play 151, 152, 153, 170, 174, 175;
    stores 155
Graphics 2.0 181

Hungarian Notation 159

"if" statements 24, 28
images 53–6; dynamic 54–6;
    standard 54
image sheets 54, 106–9
imageSuffix table 55, 129
images with sprites 105–11; create an
    image sheet with texture packer
    108–9; create image sheet manually
    107–8; display and animate sprites
    109–11; image sheets 106–7
In-App Purchases 150–4
installation: Corona Editor 8–9;
    Corona SDK 8; Corona SDK for
    Mac OS X 8; Package Control
    Plugin 8; SKD for Windows 8;
    Sublime 8
Integrated Development
    Environment 8
iPhone 4 54, 129, 142
iPhone 5 129, 130, 142
iPhone 6 129, 142

JavaScript Object Notation see JSON
jpeg 54
JSON (JavaScript Object Notation)
    144–7; jsonContent 146; jsonFile 146

Kindle Fire 140

letterBox 137
level 18, 144, 161
lines (shape) 58, 59
lists 31–2; browse 32; create 31–2;
    remove from 32
logo 129
loop statements 25–6; "break" 26; "for"
    25, 28, 30; "while" 25–6, 28
Lua: arrays and lists 30–3; comments
    4–5; control structure statements
    24–8; definition 6; functions 18–21;
    Object-Oriented Programming

36–40; scripting languages 4, 9;
    simple values 12–13; traces 5–6;
    variables, tables, and expressions
    12–16; see also

mail, Facebook, and Twitter 178–80
menu and user interface 125–37; add
    interactivity 131; add some fishes
    130; animate the menu 131–2;
    background picture 128–9; game
    logo 129; play button 129–30; retina
    display 127–8
move objects around the screen
    67–111; animate images with sprites
    105–11; frame by frame 81–6;
    interactive way 81–6; make them
    collide but not fall 97–104
multiline text 49–51
myObject 78
MyPlayer 13, 15
myResult 14

newImage 54, 55
newImageRect 128, 133
newSprite API 110, 111

Object-Oriented Programming 36–40
OnBtn function 76
onComplete 71–3, 132
onTouch 77, 117

Package Control Plugin 8
parameters 18, 19–20, 25, 31, 55,
    68, 77, 89, 110; event 118; phase
    118; self 38–9
Pettersson, Tomas 122
physics engine 88–96; addBody
    89; bouncing ball in six lines of code
    88–9; circular body 90;
    collision detection 92–4; complex
    body 90; rectangular body 89
physics without physics 98–103; which
    objects are colliding 101–2

play button 129, 131
plugins 8, 155, 181
png 54, 107, 184

record 180; sound 122
rectangles 58, 59, 60–1, 70, 74, 88
regular sounds 122, 123
resolution 44, 45, 54, 55, 128, 129, 136
Retina display 54, 127–8, 133
reverse transition 69

save and restore data 143–7; JSON file
    format 142; load data for game con-
    tent 143–4; safe and restore player
    data 147
saveToFile 147
scale 55, 70, 136–7
scaleTo 73
score 14, 18, 142
screen jungles 135–42; content area
    136–7; full screen app 137–40;
    iPhone 5 specificity 142; magical
    config.lua 141
scripting languages 4, 9
SFRX 122
shapes 57–64; circle 58–9; combining
    with text 60–4; lines 59;
    rectangle 59
sounds and music 121–4; create
    a sound 122; download or
    buy a sound 122; play a sound, the
    advanced way 123–4; play
    a sound, the straight way
    122–3
store complex values 13
store simple values 12–13
stream sounds 122–3
strings 12
Sublime Text 8, 9, 10, 15, 164

tables 13
tap event 76–7, 102, 116
test and debug 157–61; do the mon-
    key 160; internal version number
    160; learn from your mistakes 160;
    make real people test your game 160;
    pro advice to isolate bugs 161; pro
    tips to avoid bugs 159; readable 159;
    reason to 158; traces 160, 161–2; see
    also debug; XCode simulator
TestFlight 160, 173
third party plugins 181
titles 12; squared 63–4; with a back-
    ground 60–2; underlined 63
touch event 76–7, 78–9
traces 5–6, 83, 139, 160, 161–2,
    165, 166
transitions: animate more than the
    position 70–1; cancel and pause
    73; convenient methods 73–4;
    to move and animate objects 68;
    onComplete 71–3; parameters 68;
    from point to point 68; reverse 69;
    smooth 71
Twitter 178

variables 26–7; global 26; local 27;
    see also score; level, energy

"while" loop 25–6, 28
widgets 178

XCode simulator 164–5, 173
xScale 70, 74

yscale 70

zoomEven 137
zoomStretch 137